teaching and supervision

The Academic's Support Kit

Building your Academic Career
Rebecca Boden, Debbie Epstein and Jane Kenway

Getting Started on Research
Rebecca Boden, Jane Kenway and Debbie Epstein

Writing for Publication
Debbie Epstein, Jane Kenway and Rebecca Boden

Teaching and Supervision
Debbie Epstein, Rebecca Boden and Jane Kenway

Winning and Managing Research Funding
Jane Kenway, Rebecca Boden and Debbie Epstein

Building Networks
Jane Kenway, Debbie Epstein and Rebecca Boden

teaching and
supervision

Debbie **Epstein**

Rebecca **Boden**

Jane **Kenway**

SAGE Publications
London • Thousand Oaks • New Delhi

First published 2005

 SAGE Publications Ltd
1 Oliver's Yard
55 City Road
London EC1Y 1SP

SAGE Publications Inc.
2455 Teller Road
Thousand Oaks, California 91320

SAGE Publications India Pvt Ltd
B-42, Panchsheel Enclave
Post Box 4109
New Delhi 110 017

British Library Cataloguing in Publication data

A catalogue record for this book is available from the British Library

ISBN 0 7619 4232 7 (Boxed set)

Library of Congress control number available

Typeset by C&M Digitals (P) Ltd, Chennai, India
Printed in Great Britain by Cromwell Press Ltd, Trowbridge, Wiltshire

Contents

Acknowledgements

Books such as these are, inevitably, the product of the labours, wisdom and expertise of a cast of actors that would rival that of a Hollywood epic.

Our biggest thanks go to our publishers, Sage, and especially Julia Hall and Jamilah Ahmed for unswerving enthusiastic support from the very beginning and for their careful and constructive advice throughout.

We would like to thank the authors of *Publishing in Refereed Academic Journals: A Pocket Guide* and especially Miranda Hughs for her hard work and insights which led the way conceptually.

Many people reviewed the initial proposal for the *Academic's Support Kit* at Sage's request and gave it a very supportive reception. We are grateful for their early faith in us and promise to use them as referees again!

The annotated Further Reading was excellently crafted by Penny Jane Burke, Geeta Lakshmi and Simon Robb. In addition, Elizabeth Bullen gave enormous help on issues of research funding and William Spurlin helped us unravel the complexities of US universities. All are valued friends and colleagues and we appreciate their efforts.

Much of the material in the *Kit* was 'road-tested' in sessions for our postgraduate students, colleagues and others. Many other people kindly gave their time to read and comment on drafts. We are very grateful to these human guinea pigs for their hard work and can assure our readers that, as far as we are aware, none of them was harmed in the experiment.

Chris Staff of the University of Malta devised the title the *Academic's Support Kit*, and he and Brenda Murphy provided glorious Mediterranean conditions in which to write. Malmesbury, Morwell and Gozo were splendid writing localities, although Dox 'added value' at Malmesbury with his soothing yet sonorous snoring.

We are grateful to our universities – Cardiff, Monash, South Australia and the West of England – for the material support and encouragement they gave the project.

Many people in many different universities around the world inspired the books and unwittingly provided the material for our vignettes. They are too many to mention by name and besides we have had to tell their stories under other names. We are deeply indebted to our colleagues, ex-colleagues, friends, enemies, students and past students, old lovers, past and present combatants and allies and all the managers that we have ever worked with for being such a rich source of illustration and inspiration!

We particularly thank that small and select band of people who have acted as a constant source of succour and support, wise guidance and true friendship at various crucial stages of our careers: Michael Apple, Richard Johnson, Diana Leonard, Alison Mackinnon, Fazal Rizvi, Gaby Weiner, Roger Williams and Sue Willis.

Finally, as ever, our greatest thanks go to our nearest and dearest, without whose tolerance, love and hard work these books would not be in your hands today.

D.E.
R.B.
J.K.

Introducing the *Academic's Support Kit*

Before you really get into this book, you might like to know a bit more about the authors.

Rebecca Boden, from England, is professor of accounting at the University of the West of England. She did her PhD in politics immediately after graduating from her first degree (which was in history and politics). She worked as a contract researcher in a university before the shortage of academic jobs in 1980s Britain forced her into the civil service as a tax inspector. She subsequently launched herself on to the unsuspecting world of business schools as an accounting academic.

Debbie Epstein, a South African, is a professor in the School of Social Sciences at Cardiff University. She did her first degree in history and then worked briefly as a research assistant on the philosopher Jeremy Bentham's papers. Unable to read his handwriting, she went on to teach children in a variety of schools for seventeen years. She returned to university to start her PhD in her forties and has been an academic ever since.

Jane Kenway, an Australian, is professor of education at Monash University with particular responsibility for developing the field of global cultural studies in education. She was a schoolteacher and outrageous hedonist before she became an academic. But since becoming an academic she has also become a workaholic, which has done wonders for her social life, because, fortunately, all her friends are similarly inclined. Nonetheless she is interested in helping next-generation academics to be differently pleasured with regard to their work and their lives.

As you can see, we have all had chequered careers which are far from the stereotype of the lifelong academic but that are actually fairly typical. What we have all had to do is to retread ourselves, acquire new skills and learn to cope in very different environments. In our current jobs we all spend a lot of time helping and supporting people who are learning to be or developing themselves as academics. Being an accountant, Rebecca felt that there had to be a much more efficient way of helping people to get the support they need than one-to-one conversations. This book and the other five in the *Academic's Support Kit* are for all these people, and for their mentors and advisers.

We have tried to write in an accessible and friendly style. The books contain the kind of advice that we have frequently proffered our research students and colleagues, often over a cup of coffee or a meal. We suggest that you consume their contents in a similar ambience: read the whole thing through in a relaxed way first and then dip into it where and when you feel the need.

Throughout the *ASK* books we tell the stories of anonymised individuals drawn from real life to illustrate how the particular points we are making might be experienced. While you may not see a precise picture of yourself, we hope that you will be able to identify things that you have in common with one or more of our characters to help you see how you might use the book.

Pragmatic principles/principled pragmatism

In writing these books, as in all our other work, we share a number of common perceptions and beliefs.

1. Globally, universities are reliant on public funding. Downward pressure on public expenditure means that universities' financial resources are tightly squeezed. Consequently mantras such as 'budgeting', 'cost cutting', 'accountability' and 'performance indicators' have become ubiquitous, powerful drivers of institutional behaviour and academic work.

2. As a result, universities are run as corporate enterprises selling education and research knowledge. They need 'management', which is essential to running a complex organisation such as a university, as distinct from 'managerialism' – the attempted application of 'scientific management techniques' borrowed from, though often discarded by, industry and commerce. What marks managerialism out from good management is the belief that there is a one-size-fits-all suite of management solutions that can be applied to any organisation. This can lead to a situation in which research and teaching, the *raison d'etre* of universities, take second place to managerialist fads, initiatives, strategic plans, performance

indicators and so on. Thus the management tail may wag the university dog, with the imperatives of managerialism conflicting with those of academics, who usually just want to research and teach well.

3. Increasingly, universities are divided into two cultures with conflicting sets of values. On the one hand there are managerialist doctrines; on the other are more traditional notions of education, scholarship and research. But these two cultures do not map neatly on to the two job groups of 'managers' and 'academics'. Many managers in universities hold educational and scholarly values dear and fight for them in and beyond their institutions. By the same token, some academics are thoroughly and unreservedly managerialist in their approach.

4. A bit like McDonald's, higher education is a global business. Like McDonald's branches, individual universities seem independent, but are surprisingly uniform in their structures, employment practices and management strategies. Academics are part of a globalised labour force and may move from country to (better paying) country.

5. Academics' intellectual recognition comes from their academic peers rather than their employing institutions. They are part of wider national and international peer networks distinct from their employing institutions and may have academic colleagues across continents as well as nearer home. The combination of the homogeneity of higher education and academics' own networks make it possible for them to develop local identities and survival strategies based on global alliances. The very fact of this globalisation makes it possible for us to write a *Kit* that is relevant to being an academic in many different countries, despite important local variations.

6. In order to thrive in a tough environment academics need a range of skills. Very often acquiring them is left to chance, made deliberately difficult or the subject of managerialist ideology. In this *Kit* our aim is to talk straight. We want to speak clearly about what some people just 'know', but others struggle to find out. Academia is a game with unwritten and written rules. We aim to write down the unwritten rules in order to help level an uneven playing field. The slope of the playing field favours 'developed' countries and, within these, more experienced academics in more prestigious institutions. Unsurprisingly, women and some ethnic groups often suffer marginalisation.

7. Most of the skills that academics need are common across social sciences and humanities. This reflects the standardisation of working practices that has accompanied the increasing managerialisation of universities, but also the growing (and welcome) tendency to work across old disciplinary divides. The *Academic's Support Kit* is meant for social scientists, those in the humanities and those in more applied or vocational fields such as education, health sciences, accounting, business and management.
8. We are all too aware that most academics have a constant feeling of either drowning in work or running ahead of a fire or both. Indeed, we often share these feelings. Nevertheless, we think that there *are* ways of being an academic that are potentially less stressful and more personally rewarding. Academics need to find ways of playing the game in ethical and professional ways and winning. We do not advise you to accept unreasonable demands supinely. Instead, we are looking for strategies that help people retain their integrity, the ability to produce knowledge and teach well.
9. University management teams are often concerned to avoid risk. This may lead to them taking over the whole notion of 'ethical behaviour' in teaching and research and subjecting it to their own rules, which are more to do with their worries than good professional academic practice. In writing these books, we have tried to emphasise that there are richer ethical and professional ways of being in the academic world: ways of being a public intellectual, accepting your responsibilities and applying those with colleagues, students and the wider community.

And finally ...

We like the way that Colin Bundy, Principal of the School of Oriental and African Studies in London and previously Vice-Chancellor of the University of the Witwatersrand in Johannesburg, so pithily describes the differences and similarities between universities in such very different parts of the world. Interviewed for the *Times Higher Education Supplement* (27 January 2004) by John Crace, he explains:

> The difference is one of nuance. In South Africa, universities had become too much of an ivory tower and needed a reintroduction to the pressures

of the real world. In the UK, we have perhaps gone too far down the line of seeing universities as pit-stops for national economies. It's partly a response to thirty years of underfunding: universities have had to adopt the neo-utilitarian line of asserting their usefulness to justify more money. But we run the risk of losing sight of some of our other important functions. We should not just be a mirror to society, but a critical lens: we have a far more important role to play in democracy and the body politic than merely turning out graduates for the job market.

Our hope is that the *Academic's Support Kit* will help its readers develop the kind of approach exemplified by Bundy – playing in the real world but always in a principled manner.

Books in the *Academic's Support Kit*

The *Kit* comprises six books. There is no strict order in which they should be read, but this one is probably as good as any – except that you might read *Building your Academic Career* both first and last.

Building your Academic Career encourages you to take a proactive approach to getting what you want out of academic work whilst being a good colleague. We discuss the advantages and disadvantages of such a career, the routes in and the various elements that shape current academic working lives. In the second half of the book we deal in considerable detail with how to write a really good CV (résumé) and how best to approach securing an academic job or promotion.

Getting Started on Research is for people in the earlier stages of development as a researcher. In contrast to the many books available on techniques of data collection and analysis, this volume deals with the many other practical considerations around actually doing research – such as good ways to frame research questions, how to plan research projects effectively and how to undertake the various necessary tasks.

Writing for Publication deals with a number of generic issues around academic writing (including intellectual property rights) and then considers writing refereed journal articles, books and book chapters in detail as well as other, less common, forms of publication for academics. The aim is to demystify the process and to help you to become a confident, competent, successful and published writer.

Teaching and Supervision looks at issues you may face both in teaching undergraduates and in the supervision of graduate research students. This book is not a pedagogical instruction manual – there are plenty of those around, good and bad. Rather, the focus is on presenting explanations and possible strategies designed to make your teaching and supervision work less burdensome, more rewarding (for you and your students) and manageable.

Winning and Managing Research Funding explains how generic university research funding mechanisms work so that you will be better equipped to navigate your way through the financial maze associated with various funding sources. The pressure to win funding to do research is felt by nearly all academics worldwide. This book details strategies that you might adopt to get your research projects funded. It also explains how to manage your research projects once they are funded.

Building Networks addresses perhaps the most slippery of topics, but also one of the most fundamental. Despite the frequent isolation of academic work, it is done in the context of complex, multi-layered global, national, regional and local teaching or research networks. Having good networks is key to achieving what you want in academia. This book describes the kinds of networks that you might build across a range of settings, talks about the pros and cons and gives practical guidance on networking activities.

1 Who should Use this Book and How?

The purpose of this book is to help you understand the academic teaching process better, including supervising research students' dissertations and theses. If this is the first book in the *Academic's Support Kit* that you are reading, you may find it useful to read 'Introducing the *Academic's Support Kit*'.

What are we aiming at?

We aim to help you establish sound practices and approaches to teaching and supervising that will stand you in good stead for the rest of your university teaching career. This book is not about the basics of teaching. It doesn't tell you how to do such things as develop courses, plan your classes, assess students or give tips about different ways of making your teaching more interesting. There is an ample number of books available that do this and we mention some of the best of them in our Further Reading section. Rather, it concerns:

- Good educational practice, helping you to think conceptually about your identity as a teacher, your own professional practice and the teaching environment within your institution.
- Some of the pressures that university teachers worldwide are under (and some tips on how to deal with them).
- How to develop your portfolio of teaching experiences so that you can both find out what you are good at and what you enjoy and demonstrate that you are a fully rounded teaching professional.
- How to become a good supervisor of students' research projects, particularly at postgraduate level.

Why might you find this book useful?

This book will be especially useful for you if you are:

- A research student of some sort. You may be doing some teaching yourself, in which case you will find Chapters 1–3 useful. You will certainly have a supervisor or adviser for your own studies, and Chapters 4 and 5 should give you some insight into the sort of help you can expect or demand and a different perspective on the process you are going through.
- Someone in their first academic job. This may be your first 'proper' job or you may have made a recent career change.
- Someone who is a casual (sessionally or hourly paid) teacher in a university who would like to develop an academic career in the full sense.
- Someone who has already done some teaching but who is anxious to reflect on or improve their professional practice.
- Someone who is beginning to supervise postgraduate research students or who wishes to develop their professional practice in this area further.
- A more experienced academic who is mentoring someone in one or more of these categories.

Throughout the book we will tell the stories of people, drawn from real life, to illustrate how the particular points we are making might be experienced by different sorts of individuals. While you may not see a precise picture of yourself, we hope that you will be able to identify things that you have in common with one or more of our characters to help you see how you might use the book.

First of all, we want to introduce you to some characters who are in the kind of position we think will lead them to find this book useful.

Charlie left school at eighteen and did professional training as an accountant. He then went abroad and spent twenty-seven years working as an accountant in an African country. He decided on a career change in his fifties and returned to the UK, where he obtained a bursary to study first for a research training masters and then for a doctorate.

▶

▶ One of the conditions of his bursary is that he undertakes some limited first-year undergraduate teaching that is carefully structured for him. Whilst the teaching is well within his area of professional competence as an accountant, he suffers from the dual handicap of never having taught and never having been a university student.

Maria is a university teacher of some years standing. Comparatively recently she has become research-active and embarked on her own doctorate. Doing research has made her think more critically about the nature of knowledge, the purpose of universities and her role in teaching. In addition, she voluntarily undertook a postgraduate teaching qualification within her university, which successfully facilitated her development as a reflexive teacher. She is still relatively junior in her department and has suffered interference in her teaching from more senior colleagues that is at odds with her new-found insights into the teaching and learning process. At a personal level, she cares deeply about students and is much loved by them. As an ethnic minority member of staff in a predominantly white university, she is extremely aware of social justice issues and has had to contend with racism at work herself.

Joan was always a highly successful student. She won a scholarship to follow a doctoral course at an Ivy League university in the USA. During her course, like other doctoral students, she became a Teaching Assistant. She was responsible for all aspects of teaching, its organisation and student assessment and progression, with the exception of defining the curriculum content and delivering the big lectures. Her university provided virtually no training or guidance for her or other TAs in how to do this work.

William was a mature student who, after gaining his first degree, was retained by his institution to do some casual sessional teaching. Because William and his wife also ran a business, he was under little ▶

▶ pressure to develop a professional career after graduating. He stayed in this casual employment role for six years and was relied upon and, indeed, exploited by his department to do a raft of unpopular and low-level teaching jobs. Nobody offered him any training or development for a number of years. Eventually he badgered the dean into allowing him to go on a short training course provided by the university for casual teaching staff. He also insisted that the university pay him to do so. He enjoyed this course and it gave him a renewed sense of professional competence and confidence. He then persuaded the university to pay him to do a research training masters and, as part of that, he set about researching the use of casualised staff by universities.

Saskia has been a university lecturer for some time. She is quite well established as a researcher because she has published in refereed journals, co-authored a book and is on the editorial board of a major international journal. However, she began her PhD quite a long time after she got her first academic job and is only now coming close to finishing it. She hopes to hand it in within the next three months and is anxious to begin supervising doctoral students as soon as possible, both for the enjoyment of the work and for her own professional career development.

You may:

- Want to further develop your thinking about your teaching: for most academics (quite rightly, we think) a successful career still encompasses both research and teaching, and you need to be skilled in both.
- Be under tremendous institutional pressure to teach more, to document and justify your teaching more and to 'objectively' prove that you are a 'successful' teacher.
- Be someone who is really dissatisfied with the notions of teaching and learning that are increasingly promulgated and enforced by the management of mass higher education institutions who are anxious to implement pedagogic systems that are marketised, measurable and auditable. You may want to develop a critical conceptual tool-box for reflecting on your place in such a system.

Whatever your motivation in reading this, you've almost certainly done some teaching already. Many academics cut their teaching teeth while they are doctoral students. Such people undertake teaching not only to earn much-needed cash to support themselves but also to start to learn how to teach in higher education. Those academics who have come into universities after a previous professional career may well have experience as sessional teachers on professional courses or have worked as teaching assistants in a university. Some may have taught children in schools or young people in post-compulsory colleges outside higher education.

What's our position on university teaching?

Whatever your experience to date, academics have traditionally learned to teach on the job and have received little or no formal training in how to teach. The quality of much higher education teaching has, consequently, tended to be variable. We have all had experience of truly excellent university teachers, and of really terrible ones. One of the advantages of this somewhat shambolic approach was that it allowed real creativity to blossom, sometimes in places where you wouldn't expect it. On the other hand, students were sometimes ill served by their teachers and did not have good or valuable learning experiences.

Increasingly universities are engaged in strategic 'risk management'. In theory this is about balancing risks against opportunities presented by innovation and entrepreneurial activity. The unfortunate reality is that 'risk management' generally involves an emphasis on the risks without linking them with the opportunities offered by innovation. This tends to lead to extremely risk-averse behaviour. This irrational preoccupation with the avoidance of risk has contributed to the imposition of onerous internal regulatory audit and surveillance mechanisms.

Increasingly, in countries such as the UK, the USA and Australia, universities have sought to minimise the risk of 'bad teaching'. Rather than do so by promoting reflexivity and self-regulation among academics, they have often resorted to rather crude managerialist techniques for 'ensuring quality' (sometimes known as 'quality assurance' or 'total quality management'). These regimes usually involve 'performance indicators', as we will show further in Chapter 3. Such approaches are great, they argue, because they enable league tables and other comparative devices to be constructed so that an institution can 'prove' that it offers students a better deal.

It is important to make the point that even though we are critical of these performative practices and empty rituals of verification, we are not critical of good teaching practices. One of the reasons why these so-called quality assurance practices can achieve purchase is that they appeal to the common sense of many teachers and their desire to teach well. Clearly, good teachers are concerned about what students get from their teaching and the impact that they have on students' understanding, knowledge and critical engagement. Equally, good teachers are concerned to get constructive feedback from students about their teaching and their courses. However, these regimes of control don't deliver on their rhetorical promises.

Furthermore, we would argue that the systems that such managerialism has fostered run the risk of squeezing out good and imaginative teaching practice and removing the real joy of pedagogic relations. Worse still, the kinds of approach to teaching that allow risk reduction and measurement are nearly always the worst kinds of teaching. They bear no relation to how people learn, to the unpredictability of the best classrooms and learning experiences, or to the importance of teacher–student relations in the teaching and learning process. What this means is that insistence on tying teaching to what can be measured actually institutes and produces poor pedagogy.

This regime of control puts professional teachers in a bind over what they are empowered to do. It encourages and promotes a regime of self-discipline that doesn't only control our teaching but also controls who we are as professionals. The neurotic pressures that can result from being forced into poor pedagogical practices can prevent people from enjoying their teaching. Rather like the move from craft production to factory manufacture, teaching stops being a creative act and becomes a series of boring chores done under rigid surveillance. The problem is that the whole regime is set up in such a way that it can feel as if there's no other way of thinking about teaching. There appears to be no other discourse – that is, ways of thinking, speaking or acting – about teaching available.

There are a number of additional pressures, which arise from such things as the reduction in public spending on higher education and associated marketisation and commercialisation of everything universities do. These include the overt and covert pressure to do some or all of the following things:

- Admit inappropriately qualified students to courses and programmes.
- Pass students who clearly should fail.
- Overlook plagiarism.
- Adjust course content to meet the demands of external bodies when it conflicts with maintaining the academic integrity of the course.
- Dumb courses down.
- Inappropriate accreditation of prior experience.
- Double-count previous study at a lower level.
- Inflate grades beyond what the work merits.

These are profoundly anti-educational moves and have no place in a university.

In this context, it is particularly important for academics to retain critical reflexivity about teaching. If you are in a situation where your teaching is controlled by one of these managerialist systems, you do need to be able to play the game competently if you are to survive as an academic. But it's critically important not to lose sight of the fact that it is a game, with rules, and that there are alternative ways of teaching. Remember that, as in any other controlling regime, you do still have professional standing and room to manoeuvre. Indeed, your room to move can arise from your professional standing and you need to take responsibility for that.

In sum, with regard to these controls over your teaching, we would urge you not to:

- *Over-comply.* Do the bare minimum to meet the requirements and concentrate your energies and efforts on ensuring that your teaching is as good and imaginative as it can possibly be.
- *Be intimidated* into believing that the consequences of minimal but sufficient compliance will be devastating.
- *Ever believe that this is the way to improve your teaching.* It's important to maintain a critical distance between what you believe to be good teaching and what these audit systems are saying.

In *Star Trek* there is an on-going story of the Borg, an alien entity who are trying to take over the universe, species by species. The Borg have no individuality and they take over other civilisations by ▶

▶ absorbing the minds and memories of each species member that they meet. The individuals thus absorbed lose their individuality and have cyborg implants that have to be regenerated at regular intervals. They work as a hive, and the individuals become 'drones', unable to think for themselves. In *The Next Generation* the Borg absorb Captain Picard, but his crew manage to free him and he manages to stop himself behaving and acting like a drone. In *Voyager* a Borg drone, Seven of Nine, joins the crew. She is integrated into the crew and gradually learns to be an individual. The Borg's catch phrase is 'Resistance is futile'. The stories of Captain Picard and of Seven demonstrate that, far from being futile, resistance can be extremely effective. We leave you to draw your own conclusions as to why we think this story is a good analogy.

We can't change the world and we realise that some of you may feel very vulnerable in terms of your employment. But in this book we can help you to think about how you can devise ways to minimise the bad effects of this sort of managerialist control, to find ways through the 'quality maze' and to maintain your integrity and ethical practice as a teacher. And remember that in your own institution there are likely to be academics all the way up the hierarchy who are equally critical, if not more so, of these regimes and who have found ways to teach well despite them.

We need to remember that the introduction of managerialist teaching quality control systems was made easy by the fact that academic teachers themselves generally did not have a well articulated sense of professional teaching practice. This was reprehensible. It's all very well criticising the new systems, but we have to give serious consideration to what we would like to develop in their place. This is a professional responsibility incumbent on us all.

What does a good university teacher look like?

It is likely that, even if you have done almost no teaching in the past, you already have some of the relevant skills for successful teaching. To be an excellent university teacher you will need:

- First-rate interpersonal and communication skills.
- Superior observational skills in order to be aware of how your students are reacting in class, how they are progressing and what their problems are.
- Excellent presentational skills, the ability to put a point across and to make people interested in what you have to say. This may require a level of acting skill. You certainly have to have 'presence'.
- Well honed innovative problem-solving skills, because every teaching situation is different and you have to be able to think on your feet and work your way through new and complex situations.
- The ability to listen and to facilitate the learning of others. This means shaping and steering the classroom space, not dominating it.
- An understanding of the processes by which, and situations in which, people are able to learn.
- Enthusiasm for working with others to achieve your goals.
- The ability to organise yourself, manage your own work and plan ahead.
- The capacity to meet and seek out new challenges without feeling (too) intimidated.
- To be knowledgeable about what you teach and why you teach it.
- To be excited by the material you are teaching and really engaged with it. This is why we think that the best university teachers are also active researchers.
- To be able to read, digest, summarise and synthesise complex material and help others understand it.
- Imagination and the ability to be creative about how you explain things and how you get students to engage with your material.
- Curiosity and an enquiring mind.
- A real, conscious awareness of power dynamics and a good sense of social justice.
- An attitude to students which is distinguished by care and concern for their educational welfare, but conversely keeps proper boundaries and emphasises that ultimately students are responsible for their own learning.
- An understanding of the potentially transformative, and sometimes personally disruptive, effects of good education on students.

This is a pretty exhaustive (not to say exhausting) and intimidating list. Nobody scores full marks all the time and all good, reflexive academics go on developing these sorts of skills throughout their careers. Done well, teaching is hard work. It is tiring and demanding in physical, intellectual and emotional ways. It can also give enormous pleasure, joy and a sense of fulfilment and a job well done. Good teachers learn from their students in a whole host of different ways. And students are usually amazingly appreciative of good teaching and very loyal to good teachers.

2 Teaching Relations

In this chapter we discuss the three overlapping and interlinking sets of relations that being a university teacher involves: with students, with colleagues (both academic and administrative) and with university managers. Relations with external partners such as professional accreditation bodies or employers are discussed in *Building Networks*, so we will not consider them here. It is important to learn how to operate and survive successfully in all these sets of relationships, for in a sense, successful teaching is about good relationships.

Relations with students

It may seem obvious, but it needs saying: students are the most important people to think about in relation to your teaching. There is a tendency, in the marketised university system, to think of students as 'customers'. We regard this as dangerous thinking. The fact that students may have to pay fees to attend your courses does not make them 'customers' or even 'clients'. Students are people whose job it is to study and learn. It is the job of teachers to make that possible for them in the best ways they can. With their fees they do not purchase knowledge to be poured into them as if they were empty vessels to be filled. Instead they pay for access to the institution and its staff, libraries and other resources that will enable them to work at acquiring knowledge and personal growth.

Calling students 'customers' encourages them, colleagues and university management to regard them as participants in a commercial commodity exchange contract. It discourages everyone from viewing students as people who have to take responsibility for their own learning and as active agents in their own right. It is also delusional because students as 'customers' actually have no consumer rights. All they can do, if they don't like what they get, is sue or go to another institution. Neither of these options is likely to be to their educational advantage.

Lianna is a doctoral student undertaking some casually paid teaching. She has previously trained as a school teacher. She is always anxious to ensure that students are active participants in the seminar classes that she runs. One day she asked a truculent young man if he knew the answer to a particular question that had been raised. He replied, 'No. I pay fees here. You are supposed to give me the answers.' Lianna, a mother of young children, contained her exasperation and took a great deal of time and effort to explain to this callow youth where his attitude to education had gone wrong.

If we believe that the notion of a customer–contractor relationship between students and teachers is not helpful to anyone, how should we conceptualise these relationships?

The characteristics of good pedagogic relationships

When your teaching is good, it is likely that you will derive a great deal of pleasure from the process. Good pedagogy generally has the following characteristics, to a greater or lesser extent:

- Students are regarded as ultimately responsible for their own learning, and as individuals – even in classes which are too large for us to know them all individually.
- There is mutual respect and regard between teachers and students and among students themselves. The kind of attitude that allows one to think of students as 'thick' or 'stupid' has no place in teaching, as it connotes lack of respect or regard for individuals and an abrogation of responsibilities in the teaching relationship.
- Courses and lessons are well planned, but allow for the unexpected and for students to take some control over the process. This does not mean that teachers always do what students want them to, but it does mean that our reasons for doing things in a particular way are explicit, explained and justified.
- Relationships are built over time and classes develop a group dynamic all their own which includes their relationship with the teacher. In this way students and teachers feel as if they are part of a collective endeavour in which the teacher may have the route map but the

students can also look at it and make suggestions for alternative routes, modes of transport and, indeed, where on the map they wish to end up as a group and/or as individuals. In other words, the outcomes of any healthy learning process cannot, by definition, be predetermined by teachers alone or by external agents. The outcomes depend on a whole raft of different things, for example: the relationship between teachers and students; the group dynamics of the class; what the students bring to the class before the course starts; how much work students put in; and what they want to take away from it.

- Team teaching can be an extremely successful way of running courses, but it does not obviate the responsibility of the staff to ensure that students experience continuity and a real sense of collective class identity. We would therefore recommend that there is always at least one teacher who pretty much stays with the group from the first to the last class.

- Power relations are recognised, not only between teachers and students, but between different students. This should allow teachers and students to take joint responsibility for ensuring that there is no bullying, exclusion, abuse or exploitation. It is, however, the teacher who must keep on top of this and therefore the teacher has a special responsibility in this regard.

Hannah was teaching a small class in a British university that consisted of white British men and a group of Malaysian Chinese women. The women had recently arrived in the UK and had received no induction into Western pedagogic conventions. Hannah had noticed that they were reluctant to contribute to group discussions and were painfully shy. She organised the class into small sub-groups for an exercise and told them to appoint a rapporteur. At the end of the exercise, she asked one group, consisting of two men and three women, for their rapporteur's feedback. One of the men immediately said, 'One of them' (pointing at the silent women) 'should do it, because they never do or say anything.' Hannah replied, 'As you are so discourteous, I think you should do it,' and made him be the rapporteur. She spoke to the young man privately immediately after the class and asked him to reflect on his hostile attitude towards young women who probably needed his friendship and support as a fellow student.

In contrast, positive relationships with students are put at risk when:

- Teaching is seen as the delivery of prepackaged nuggets of information to students as customers. This undermines the crucial role of the teacher in developing these all-important relationships with students. Teachers aren't delivery systems that can be replaced at will by someone else or by a Web-based teaching package. Those universities which specialise in distance learning usually know this well and take a great deal of care to ensure that students have a sense of belonging and that they have a real relationship with a real person, albeit at a distance.
- Commercialised customer–contractor relations are put in place. In these circumstances students and teachers are set in conflict with each other. This undermines any sense of mutual trust. It is incumbent on teachers, we believe, to reach out to students and to form mutually beneficial alliances. In our model of education, students and teachers are partners or collaborators in the same endeavours. If they are driven apart the only people who benefit are those who seek to control the education process for their own purposes.

Rebecca was teaching a class of final-year Management Studies undergraduates. She asked them how they were getting on generally. They immediately started complaining that they didn't get very good 'service' from the university and about how much they resented paying their fees. Rebecca explained that, when she was a student in the 1970s, such upset would have led students to occupy the administration building. This was not their style. So Rebecca pointed out that they were in part the authors of their own misfortune: misguidedly thinking of themselves as 'customers' with 'consumer rights'. She suggested that they could do better for themselves by acting as real members of a collegiate community and exercising their legitimate voice. The next week the same students asked her how they could get to see the dean. She told them, but cautioned them to have a well worked out case, as they would be dismissed out of hand if they whinged to the dean in the same way they had whinged to her. In the end, the students turned up at faculty board with a closely argued and professional PowerPoint presentation. The faculty managers acceded to their reasonable requests. The students learned a valuable life lesson.

Relations with colleagues

Working with other academics

In teaching we often have to work with, alongside and sometimes for colleagues. We always have to work together to operate the routine systems of the administration that supports teaching. Clearly, in a university students have to be selected, recruited, registered, assessed and graded. We think that the more these processes are controlled by academics the better. Whilst it may be tempting for you and your colleagues to accept the kind offer of the university management to deal with applications for your programmes, beware Trojan horses. What can often happen in such situations is that you lose control, for instance, over the number, nature and quality of students admitted to your pro-gramme, to people who neither know nor care about what matters to you as a professional teacher and whose chief concern is to maximise income and justify their own jobs. This is not to say that you should take on basic, routinised clerical work – your task is to help to develop policy, decide strategic directions and oversee their implementation.

The more pressure we come under as academics, the more important it becomes to be and to have good colleagues. A good colleague might answer the following questions in the affirmative.

Am I a good team player?

By this we mean that good colleagues are able to take the wider view, taking account of the good of the department, faculty and university as a whole and not just of their own little corner or self-interest. This can be quite difficult in situations of straitened resources and near-intolerable work pressures. But in our experience, once academic institutions descend into dog-eat-dog behaviour, they are doomed and the people in them become very miserable. Moreover, it is hard for institutions to recover from such negative behaviour patterns and traditions.

Toby belonged to a teaching team consisting of some really high-flying academics. Toby did not have a research qualification and was not doing any research. He felt vulnerable and defensive in ▶

▶ consequence. His way of dealing with his feeling of inadequacy was to comment pejoratively on the intellectual content of the course. In tutorials and one-to-one sessions with students he sought to discredit his colleagues' material and approach by constructing them as 'airy-fairy ivory-tower' academics and himself as a 'real practitioner' with the only valuable insights. Behaviour such as Toby's may unwittingly endorse the anti-intellectual trends that we discussed earlier.

Am I flexible?

That is, in their work practices good colleagues will accommodate the needs and problem of others the best they can. For instance, they would not insist on continuing to teach a particular course when a less experienced and more junior colleague wanted and needed the experience of that particular kind of teaching. By the same token, they are not doormats, ever willing to bend over backwards to accommodate unreasonable expectations.

Susannah shared the teaching of a course for a particular group of part-time students with another colleague. The students attended the university one day a week, starting at 8.30 p.m. and ending at 9.00 p.m. Susannah had sole responsibility for two young children whom she had to either take to/collect from school herself or make complex arrangements for someone else to. Her co-teacher was a middle-aged childless man with no such domestic responsibilities. He was in charge of allocating the teaching and gave himself the teaching slots in the middle of the day, leaving Susannah to teach from 8.30 a.m. to 11.30 a.m. and 7.00 p.m. to 9.00 p.m. This, obviously, left her with insuperable childcare problems and was really quite unjust to her children. Susannah's representations to her colleague fell on deaf ears. She eventually went to her research mentor (another woman), who raised the matter with the head of department. He was sympathetic and intervened to give Susannah a more acceptable teaching schedule.

Do I carry my fair share of teaching and related administration?

The distribution, by volume and nature, of teaching and administration duties should reflect, to some degree, the levels of experience and expertise of the staff in any department. However, the allocation of teaching should be informed by a good staff development strategy and under-pinned by principles of equity.

Ideally, staff in their first teaching post should be given partial remission of teaching duties, since preparation takes so much longer when you are teaching for the first time. Unfortunately, many depart-ments do not have a sufficiently good staff–student ratio to allow this to happen to the extent that it should. However, in good departments the allocation of teaching duties and the justification for them are the subject of a transparent process.

Often more junior colleagues get put upon in a number of ways. They may have a disproportionate share of the teaching burden, get less choice of what they teach, be allocated teaching which is less enjoyable or career-enhancing or have to constantly prepare for new courses. This is bad practice and damages people's careers.

If you feel that you are in this position, you have a number of courses of action open to you. Your first recourse might be to your mentor and/or head of department. You will need to have a well argued case, not just a whinge. If that doesn't work, you may wish to take the matter up at greater length in your staff performance appraisal or review. A final recourse might be to your trade union.

Am I respectful of my colleagues, sensitive to the demands on them, and do I avoid draining their time and energy on trivia?

They will, however, ask for help when they need it. Every academic, no matter how they act, or what they say, experiences periods of extreme and near intolerable stress. You need to be aware that your colleagues may be feeling like this and, where appropriate, give them what assistance you can. The positions might well be reversed at some point in the future. However, avoid – and avoid being – the type of needy colleague who represents an unwarranted and wearisome drain on those around them. You cannot be your colleagues' mother and they cannot be yours.

> Dina is a compulsive over-achiever and regularly says 'yes' to demands that she really doesn't have time to deliver on. Failure to deliver feeds her tendency to think of herself as a failure. Things reached crisis point, with unmet deadlines looming. She had lunch with a sympathetic colleague and friend and ended up bursting into tears about her work load. Her colleague took charge of the situation by encouraging Dina to list all her outstanding tasks on the whiteboard in the office. She then made time to come to Dina's office to discuss each task in turn in order to decide which ones could be ignored, which could be handed over to someone else, and how to prioritise the remainder. She also made Dina a large notice to pin above her desk that said, 'LEARN TO SAY NO!'

Do I appropriately prioritise my own teaching, research and administrative responsibilities?

Colleagues who ignore their own work in order to do things for other people are actually more of a burden than a benefit. Those who unnecessarily create work for others to do fail to respect the needs of others to get on with their own work.

> Boubacar and Achille were two hard-working, research-active but junior academics who shared an office. Both devoted considerable effort to their teaching work and were always ready to support each other and their students, who felt that they were given a very good deal. Leela was their new head of department and a relatively inexperienced academic.
> Leela came into Boubacar and Achille's office one day. She explained that her understanding was that the whole department had to convene a special meeting in order to review the quality of the ▶

▶ course 'Quality' documents produced by each individual member of staff. Incredulous, Boubacar and Achille suggested making the minutes of such a meeting up or, less flippantly, that this rather pointless procedure should be tacked on to the end of their regular departmental meetings with separate minutes being produced. Leela insisted that the meeting had to be specially convened. She told Boubacar and Achille that she could make the meeting on any day except Tuesdays and asked them when they were free. Achille replied, without a moment's hesitation, 'Tuesdays.'

Both Boubacar and Achille have now got jobs at other institutions and others in their erstwhile department are seeking to make similar moves.

Do I avoid setting up unrealistic and inappropriate expectations of what teaching staff will do?

Like the rest of us, students generally want an easy life. The more you do for them, the happier they are, and the less they do for themselves the more they resent those teachers who do not spoonfeed them. To spoonfeed students does not help them to become mature and independent learners who take responsibility for themselves and their own learning.

The imposition of student evaluation surveys in universities may have the unfortunate and unintended effect of encouraging some teachers to court popularity by falling over backwards to do things for students where it is not appropriate and not to the students' long-term benefit. Such activities include: putting your lectures on the intranet so that your on-campus students don't have to bother to come to your classes; being endlessly available to see students who have missed your classes because of their own recalcitrance or lack of personal organisation; setting easy assessment tasks that are not challenging and are also subject to lax grading; giving students endless tutorials above and beyond what is appropriate in order to help them get through or raise their grades; bending the rules around registration, assessment or progression.

Of course some situations do arise where special consideration is due to specific students who, through no fault of their own, have encountered difficulties. However, such treatment of students should not become part of regular teaching practice and teachers should not be seen as a 'soft touch' by self-serving students. This sort of conduct by teachers is not only detrimental to students' real interests, but also undermines the best teaching practice of their colleagues. It can put your colleagues in an invidious position if they are faced with a student who is protesting, 'But Dr Bush *always* does this.'

Working with academic support staff

Finally, we want to mention teachers' relations with those colleagues who support and facilitate so much of the work done by academics. Many of them are supportive, caring, efficient and committed colleagues. Particularly worthy of praise, we think, are librarians. It is imperative to work well with all these people and that you treat them with respect, work with them co-operatively, recognise their skills and make sure they can do their job effectively.

Nestor is an administrative officer to a Dean of Research in a large division (faculty) in a sizeable university. The dean wanted to encourage honours students to understand the pathways that existed for them to undertake postgraduate study. Rather than assuming that she needed to give Nestor detailed instructions about how to undertake this piece of work, she was able to delegate to Nestor complete responsibility for organising a special evening, including everything from room bookings to recruiting and briefing speakers (not choosing them) and maximising student attendance. When she congratulated Nestor on the success of the event, the dean discovered that she had substantial experience of organising such events in her previous job.

Efficiently undertaken, the work of such people can be invaluable in supporting the academic work process. Often they know their way round the rules and systems really well and can help you achieve your legitimate objectives with the minimum fuss. Such people are well worth cultivating as friends and colleagues too. Do not assume that all your university friendships will be with academic staff.

Vashti is the research manager of a large and successful business school. She is responsible for all aspects of procedural research support such as helping with grant applications, organising conferences and for all the administrative aspects of a large graduate research degrees programme. Her job is complex, beset by many and confusing regulations and involves interaction with over eighty academics and more than forty research students. Her job involves working alongside two senior academics: the Director of Research and the Director of Research Degrees.

The fact that Vashti has a PhD, albeit in ancient history, means that she has a real and deep understanding of both the research process and what it means to be a research student. In doing her work she is confident, assertive and makes her own distinct and valuable contribution. Yet, at the same time, she implicitly acknowledges that her job is to facilitate the research and teaching of the academics, not to tell them what to do. As such, she is a valued and highly respected colleague.

An example of her contribution is that, under university regulations, there must be a body of definitive and quite complex documentation relating to the research degree programmes. When Vashti took up her post, this was sadly out of date and neglected. Without being asked, Vashti set about collecting and collating the relevant information and identifying gaps and areas where updating was necessary. When she had completed her first draft, she arranged a meeting with the Director of Research Degrees. They reviewed her draft together and decided how it could be finalised. Vashti finalised the document and took it through the relevant committees for approval.

Whinging or critique?

As will be clear, by now, we believe that academics have a lot to put up with. However, it doesn't help anyone if we spend our time endlessly whinging, moaning and complaining. All that does is exhaust our colleagues and us. We would wish to distinguish, here, between whingeing and critique. Critique is about analysing (rigorously, theoretically and conceptually) why we want to whinge. Whereas whinging drains positivity and leads to individual and organisational paralysis, critique is empowering for you and also for those you share it with provided that you build on it and turn it into positive alternatives.

Let us take the case of the intensification of teaching and the burgeoning of bureaucracy and the implications they have for research activity. A whinger would simply complain endlessly and uselessly to anyone who would listen about the impossibility of their work load. A critique would involve somebody identifying and understanding the structural changes that have occurred in university work practices and rendering them explicit to colleagues and their managers. A critic with a sense of the possible would take the critique and find imaginative and positive ways of resolving the problems, to mutual benefit. For instance, rather than go to their head of school with a problem, they would go with a clear definition of the problem and a precise articulation of a feasible solution.

Relations with management

The good

We would argue that that there are two sorts of people who tend to do management work well. They may be, or have been, good academics with an aptitude for management-type work. Often you find these people working as heads of department, deans and so on. Traditionally, the heads of institutions have come through this route. Alternatively, good managers are not academics but do have empathy for and intuitive understanding of academic processes and practices, and see their role very much as facilitating academic work. If the managers and management systems of your institution come from one or other (or both) of these groups, you are unlikely to have fundamental problems in your relations with them. Usually such people will be able to listen openly to you and will support your reasonable requests, particularly if these are seen to enhance both your academic activities and those of their own institutional unit. And of course they will expect you to carry your fair share of the admin. work of your school or faculty.

The bad

Unfortunately, we discern a new development in universities world-wide. It is an increasing tendency towards managerialism (as opposed to management). It is not confined to universities but, as the journalist and commentator Simon Hoggart points out in the article quoted below, is ubiquitous.

Management is seen these days as a separate concept which can be plonked on top of any organisation, whether it cures the sick or sells office supplies. Therefore managers often have nothing to do with the trade they're managing. Instead they are trained in management. This is why someone like Gerald Corbett, who knew about hotels, catering, retail shops and oil, came to run Railtrack, with results we now know very well.

Because management is seen as a good in itself, managers feel free to spread it everywhere. Frequently the methods it involves don't work, which means that more managers are required to force it to work. Managers set wages, and since they rate management very highly, managers get the fattest pay packets. This draws more people into management and away from actually doing whatever their organisation is supposed to do.

We can see the results everywhere: in the health service, the railways, our schools and the police. We're plagued with managers as they spread destruction like ground elder in a garden. *Managing Britannia* – which I need hardly add is written in a straightforward, lucid fashion – is published by Edgeways Books.

On a long train journey this week I found at one point that no fewer than five businessmen around me were using their mobile phones. I no longer find this annoying; it's just part of the background noise of modern life, like barking dogs or traffic. I now have a game: I eavesdrop and try to work out what their business actually does. As they bang on about 'delivery outcomes', 'laptop presentations', 'input assessment' and 'faxing the specs to Chris in Woking' you can almost never work out if they're in manufacturing, retail, services or anything real at all. Try it some time; you usually can't tell if they run a probation service or a lap dancing club.

Then to my great relief, the chap behind me started talking about 2.25 kilo boxes of pickled eggs. 'We need to get 5,000 boxes,' he said. 'The whole order, 17 K boxes, is riding on it.'

Pickled eggs! Something real! He sold catering supplies, and you can eat what he sells! I almost wanted to hug him.

(Simon Hoggart, 'A plague of managers spreads destruction', *Guardian*, 2 March 2002)

Managerialism reflects a very different approach to the management work of a university than the traditional mode in which it's done by academics or, as we noted, by people who see their role as facilitating the work of academics. In many OECD countries and those that are subject to strong 'reforming' pressure from organisations such as the World Bank, this tendency towards the managerialisation of universities has been encouraged, promoted or even insisted upon by government, government agencies and/or supranational agencies.

The ugly

These governmental pressures have often led to demands on universities and their academic staff that are not only aggravating and time-consuming but also expensive to operationalise. Ironically, such managerialist systems and structures are seldom subject to the same kind of performance measurement and value for money analysis that they inflict on academics.

> Barry is in charge of the graduate school of a large faculty. He is a very good 'systems man' – he likes putting policies, processes and procedures in place and usually does it well. However, he also has a tendency to overplay his hand in this respect. His systems sometimes place unnecessary and onerous burdens on staff and fail to achieve his objective of improving research 'performance'. For instance, he carefully recorded each staff member's success rate in publishing and attracting research grants and then published a league table within the faculty reporting these. Rather than inspiring and incentivising staff, it alienated and demotivated them. Further, Barry's main means of communicating with staff was via email. So rather than having a conversation with staff to alert them to what they needed to do, he would send them long diatribes explaining their failures. Barry was a research *manager* rather than a research *leader* and never attended any of the research seminars of visiting scholars, let alone those of his own colleagues.

Managerialist people tend to manage what they can measure. It is hard for those who don't have their own academic track record or any empathy with academic work to get any measure of the quality of our research. Teaching, amenable as it is to 'customer satisfaction' surveys, league tables and other performance management regimes, is a much softer target. Managerialist demands can drain your energies from teaching and research.

A word of caution about the good, the bad and the ugly

Remember that not all managers are managerialists. Further, managerialists range along a continuum from the severely performatively disordered to the mildly performatively disordered. And of course, even managers range from those who are able to develop really good management systems that support teaching and research properly to those whose heart is probably in the right place but who could not manage their way out of a paper bag. And keep in mind that all these people, no matter how sympathetic they are to academic practices and processes, also have their financial bottom line, their Key Performance Indicators, and are ultimately largely answerable up. You would be wise to find out where your managers fit in relation to the manager/ managerialist dualism and then where they sit in the range. Don't assume they are one thing or the other until you see how they behave in relation to you.

Managing the managerialists

One important thing for the early career academic is to learn to recognise the role of managerialist processes in teaching, to be able to critique them, and to devise strategies for managing your relationships in ways that protect you and allow you to maintain your professional integrity. We set out, below, some ways in which you can successfully manage managerialist actors and the managerialist systems they put in place.

First develop the right mind set

- An important basic truth to remember is that all academics are in their jobs to research and to teach well. Much else is largely tangential and will be an unwarranted drain on your energy and resources.

- Remember that institutions need good teachers and researchers, and the better you are at those things the more they are likely to want to keep you and to treat you well. Remember, also, that there is an accelerating global shortage of academic labour in a number of disciplinary areas. This can give you considerable bargaining strength when it comes to how you do your job.
- If you can teach and research well, you will also have the moral high ground when it comes to responding to pointless managerialist tasks and unwarranted demands on your time and energies.
- You should put in place procedures that enable you to fulfil your proper teaching obligations. These should be workable for you and should not impact adversely on your other obligations (research and your fair share of committee work) and your colleagues.
- You need to develop the confidence to know that you are a professional and the self-knowledge that the managerialist actor who is trying to tell you what to do probably couldn't do your job, although you could almost certainly do theirs.

'Acts of resistance' (and a salute to Pierre Bourdieu!)

- If compliance does not conflict with your professional values or ethical practice as a teacher (or researcher) you should not resist just for the sake of it. What you should always try to do is comply in ways that enhance your teaching and research, and to do so in a way that involves the minimum time and effort.
- However, it is sad, but true, that the more people comply with bureaucratic regimes designed to enforce control and surveillance over individuals, the more power such regimes accumulate. Yet academics, especially those in the early stages of their career, may feel uneasy about the prospect of saying 'no' to managerialism's and managerialists' unreasonable demands.
- *Always* take time to think before you agree to do things. Sometimes the requests will be reasonable and helpful to you and/or colleagues, students or the institution. However, be aware that many requests are made without any real thought as to the utility of the work or care for your efforts. Consequently, when people ask you to do something, never say 'yes' or 'no' immediately; always employ a delaying tactic such as 'I have to check my diary and I'll get back to you' because that will give you time to think about whether you want to do it or not.

Remember the vignette about Dina bursting into tears because she said 'yes' too often? Well, no more. She and her partner, also an academic, have devised a game they call 'No-tivation'. It works like this. Basically, each time you say 'no' to any piece of work, request or management demand that does not evidently contribute to your research, teaching, career development or the well-being of your colleagues or students, you are awarded one or more 'No-tivation Points'. Every time you get to ten, your partner has to buy or make you a treat. You might get taken out to dinner or have the ironing done for you. The bigger the 'no' the more the points.

It is safe to try this at home. It doesn't matter if your partner isn't an academic – they may rather like a better balanced you or they may have similar issues in their own job. If you don't have a partner, you can play the game yourself, making sure that you are amply rewarded with appropriate treats. Or you could play it with a friend in your own or another academic institution.

- You should not allow yourself to be pushed around. Of course, you have to be careful about the ways in which you choose to resist unreasonable demands from managerialist actors. We try not to pick fights we can't win unless we feel, on a particular issue, that it is a ditch we are prepared to die in. You need to pick your ground carefully and to keep your self-protection antennae out.
- If non-compliance is not an option, and compliance would be compromising, it's a good idea to make any engagement with you costly in time and other resources for the managerialists.

Zhand's colleague Arjun did not come up to the standard of research activity demanded by their institution. Accordingly, he had carved out a role for himself in charge of 'teaching quality'. The university had gratefully acceded to this self-appointed role as it couldn't get anyone else to do the job. Arjun decided that it was essential for all staff to display a complete weekly schedule of where they were and what they were doing on a special notice board outside their office doors. This was designed to maximise staff availability for student consultations. Zhand ▶

▶ responded to the announcement of this scheme by pointing out that the stringent local fire regulations strictly prohibited any uncovered paper being affixed to corridor walls. He helpfully pointed out that the proposed notice boards would contravene these regulations, creating a health and safety hazard and putting the university at risk of prosecution by the fire authorities. Arjun agreed with her analysis. He spent four working days researching the availability of special notice boards covered in Perspex. He had these notice boards installed at great expense to the university. Most staff never used them because, they maintained, they were unable to get the fireproof covers off.

- You might even consider completely ignoring patently daft requests. Often they will just go away. Often the sanctions that might be exercised against you are pathetically futile and work only if you allow yourself to be bullied.

UK universities have made heroic attempts to get all academics to complete time sheets for several sample weeks, categorising time spent on various work activities. These are known as TRAC returns. Resistance to this futile process has been widespread and innovative. The sanctions for non-compliance have created hilarity across the land for those on the receiving end.

Sophie simply ignored hers, along with the majority of her colleagues in her department who had better things to do with their time. This was made easy by the fact that she was head of department. Since then she has received increasingly frantic reminders that hers and her colleagues' TRAC returns are well overdue. The sanction proposed was terrifying. She was told that 'if you don't make these returns, we'll have to keep writing to you to remind you until you do.' The forms remain uncompleted, although the staff are cowering in their offices hiding the wastepaper baskets from the administration.

Lois's institution put the TRAC returns on the intranet and asked staff to fill in their returns on-line. She complied with the first email request to make a return. She ignored the second until a reminder arrived. She ignored the third request and the subsequent two reminders. Finally the system administrator wrote to her stating that if she did not complete her return, the administrator would complete it for her. Reluctantly she allowed the administrator to do so.

- A remarkably effective form of resistance is to over-comply in minute detail. This bogs the system down so that it cannot cope with the volume of pedantic, mind-numbing requests for clarification or expressions of concern for the correct and proper operation of systems.

Here's another TRAC return story. Benjamin, an eminent mathematics professor, was so involved in his work that he used to dream mathematics and said that he thus did not know whether he was working in his sleep or not. When he got his TRAC return to fill in, he deluged the administration with requests for clarification as to what the categories meant and how he was to decide which activity fell into which box. Eventually, the administration stopped replying to him – they didn't know the answers anyway.

- Remember that no regime of control is ever total and some have more bark than bite.

Lynn is a hard-working, successful researcher and teacher in a senior position at a prestigious university. Her department is well known for driving staff to over-work. Although she regularly works well over fifty hours a week, carries a heavy administrative load, teaches her fair share and publishes extensively, the system designed to measure her work contribution suggested that she was 'underemployed'.

Her head of department called her in for a 'firm chat' about this work 'deficit'. She explained that she was working as hard as she possibly could and refused to take on any extra administrative or ▶

teaching work. The head of department said, 'But you will be in deficit.' Lynn replied, 'I'm willing to take the consequences of that,' and left the room. When asked by a friend exactly what the consequences were, she replied, 'The consequences are that the system will record that I have a workload deficit.'

We are sure that you have the imagination to think of many more modes of resistance to the more ridiculous demands made on you. The important thing is to ensure that you are safe, stay true to what you believe an academic's job is and remember that clearing the decks of useless extra bureaucratic work does not make you a bad colleague. Rather, it gives you more time, space and energy to be a good one.

And finally . . .

Clearly, all these relationships that we have outlined involve unequal inter-personal power dynamics. In this, universities are like any other large workplace. The dynamics may involve various forms of abuse, including harassment, bullying and inappropriate sexual behaviour. Most universities now recognise the existence of such behaviour and many have policies and procedures deigned to challenge it. As a member of the university you should be aware of these policies and procedures. More generally, you should not engage in such behaviour. Neither should you put up with them or be complicit with them. That said, dealing with this sort of problem is very difficult and in doing so you will need to elicit help and support from sympathetic senior staff. It's always worth tackling this sort of stuff, no matter how trivial it seems to you at the time. If inappropriate conduct is not nipped in the bud it can poison the institutional culture. This is a major health and safety issue. Universities have a legal responsibility for health and safety, and the risks associated with this sort of behaviour are ones that wise institutions wish to avoid.

In this chapter we have discussed the range of relationships that exist between you as a university teacher and your students, colleagues and managers. We now turn to the practice of teaching itself.

3   Powerful Pedagogies?

In Chapter 1 we explained our position on university teaching, placing it in a wider context. Here we expand on this, discuss the meaning of 'pedagogy', identify some institutional pressures on university teachers that make it difficult to develop good pedagogical practice and point to some ways in which good teachers have managed to get round such difficulties. We end with some brief examples of what we consider good pedagogy in context. But first we need to draw an important distinction.

We think it's vital to distinguish between training and education. Training implies equipping people for a very specific task by imparting to them, in a fairly standardised way, the relevant information or skills. It is about teaching people how to do things. Training often involves didactic pedagogic processes. In contrast, education is about helping people learn how to learn, enabling them to think critically, gain deeper knowledge and insights and ask questions to which there is not necessarily any answer – and almost certainly isn't any 'right' answer.

Education is therefore a much more slippery beast than training. This means that it is much less amenable to external control. As a result, in many parts of the world, and in many fields, education has been pushed more and more into a 'training' mode. For instance, in the UK there has been a long-standing battle between those who talk about 'initial teacher education' and successive managerialist governments, which prefer to call the process by which students become schoolteachers 'initial teacher training'. In Australia the government is promoting postgraduate 'training' whilst some universities prefer to speak of postgraduate 'education'. When we discuss pedagogy it is in relation to education, not training.

What do you mean, 'pedagogy'?

Literally 'pedagogy' means the 'science of teaching' and in most European countries people who research education and teach at university often have the title 'professor of pedagogics'. In our view, this definition of pedagogy is problematic at the outset – teaching is an art, not a science, and learning is not the result of a scientific experiment or process. Furthermore, it is a naive teacher who imagines that pedagogy is not political. Just as the production of knowledge is a political act, so is its dissemination. Contexts count, as we will now demonstrate.

In the past, people concerned about education in schools have talked, researched and written endlessly about 'learning' or about 'teaching', about the 'learner' or about the 'teacher' but seldom about both together. More recently there has been a move to think in terms of 'pedagogy', which is taken to include both learners and teachers and to encompass the dynamic relations between them. In universities, in contrast, academics have not, until recently, been overtly concerned with matters of teaching, learning or pedagogy overall. Traditionally, academics have been regarded as experts in their field, working at the cutting edge, and the assumption was that all they had to do in order to convey their knowledge to the students was to tell them about it. Little attention was paid to what students brought with them to the class – they either learnt or they didn't learn, and academics were rarely considered responsible for this. While some excellent and inspiring teaching took place, and most teaching was at least competent, there was also some lacklustre, downright poor teaching – and little was done about it. In the elite, highly selective systems that universities once were, that didn't matter much. Students were, on the whole, self-starters, competent in the languages and codes required of them and could pretty well get on with things.

Josh was a mathematics professor in an internationally renowned department. All the students had done extraordinarily well at school – particularly in mathematics – in order to get a place there. The students were disaffected and hostile in class, often talking about football, dates, or whatever, rather than paying attention to what was being taught. Josh was at the end of his tether, but didn't know what to do, particularly because he was reproducing the teaching methods that he had experienced as an undergraduate. In despair, he approached a friend who was a primary school teacher well known for her successful teaching at school level. She asked him why he thought ▶

▶ the students were so disaffected. His reply was that they did not understand the mathematics. She suggested that this might indicate a need to think about his pedagogy. He was astonished at the suggestion – it had never occurred to him that university teachers might think about pedagogy. He explained that when he was an undergraduate at another internationally renowned department he had experienced exactly the same thing. He had sat in lectures, taking notes without understanding them. Then he had gone home and worked at the examples until things clicked into place. Why couldn't his students do the same?

The move to mass systems meant that this approach became more problematic and visible because a lot of new cohorts of students became part of the system but didn't necessarily bring with them the required cultural capital. The massification of higher education was accompanied by its corporatisation and marketisation. It was at this point that the new university managerialists were able to step into the vacuum left by the inattention of academics collectively to pay sufficient attention to questions of pedagogy.

When managerialists colonise pedagogy

There is no doubt that teaching programmes in universities need to be administered and managed. Timetables, assessment, student records and so on cannot exist without management. What we refer to as problematic in this section can be regarded as 'managerialism' rather than 'management'. We noted, in Chapter 1, that managers seek to minimise the risk of 'bad teaching' through regimes of 'quality audit' and 'quality management' rather than trying to promote reflexivity among teachers. This has been reasonably easy, in part because of the relative lack of attention that academics paid to pedagogy in the past. So what have they done? And what are their buzz words? The list includes:

- Outcomes-based education.
- Flexible delivery and innovation.
- Key skills.

- Benchmarking.
- The management and measurement of learning.
- Turn-round time.
- Graduate qualities.

The list goes on and develops over time, possibly becoming less crude but remaining problematic nonetheless. Along with such lists goes increasing emphasis on the evaluation of courses and of academics through generic survey-type questionnaires, usually devised by some centrally located 'quality manager' rather than by the academics teaching the courses. Sometimes these evaluation forms are also accompanied by more general surveys designed to assess the level of student 'satisfaction' with the teacher, the course, the programme, life, the university and everything. Students may also be expected to fill in 'destination' surveys approximately six months and/or a year after graduating. The results of such surveys are seen to reflect, either positively or negatively, on degree programmes, departments and universities. In some countries they, together with student satisfaction survey results, are used by government in such a way as to influence university funding. In other countries, faculty pay is tied to the results of student evaluations and surveys. Such practices are tied to the notion of students as consumers/clients/customers, to the 'user pays' privatisation agenda of many governments and to the vocationalisation of universities.

We have no quarrel with the notion that students should provide their teachers and institution with feedback about the education and facilities the university offers. Indeed, a dialogic relationship between teachers and students is a key element in developing sound pedagogies. Equally, universities need to plan around the parameters of student demand. Our quarrel is with the managerialist methodologies and mind sets employed. Take, for instance, student evaluation of courses. Every good teacher we know has well developed ways of finding out how students are getting on, whether they understand, what they think could be improved in their courses and so on. Such evaluations are both *dialogic* and *diagnostic*. They give teachers valuable information which allows them to improve their courses and practice year on year. In contrast, the generic survey cannot, by definition, address the specificities of particular courses. Students get sick and tired of filling in the same form over and again on each course they do for three, four or five years, and become increasingly aware of how meaningless they are. In terms of improving teaching the evaluations do nothing at all. They also give students unwarranted power to harm teachers whose courses they find demanding or whose assessments aim to maintain high standards. It is so well known that students in the USA feel able to demand A grades from faculty because of this power that the problem features in such widely syndicated cartoons as *Doonesbury* – and the power can lead directly to what has become known as 'grade inflation'. In spite of these evident and indisputable problems, some universities use student evaluations as a direct and overt way of disciplining their academic staff through mechanisms of naming and shaming, as the story below shows.

The University of Woop Woop is a hyper-managerialist university. It subscribes to every new managerialist trend, fad and fancy. It treats league tables as if they were the word of God. Its senior managers' conviction is that if its teachers are named and shamed their teaching practice will improve. They have no evidence to suggest that their academic staff teach badly, but that is beside the point. They believe in the notion of Continuous Improvement through quality assurance practices. They have employed the services of external IT consultants, who have devised a program designed to keep teachers on their toes. In addition to regular evaluation surveys, students can go on to the university's intranet at any time and log in to 'evaluate' any of their courses on-line. Each course has its own virtual thermometer indicating the level of student dis/satisfaction. Even one evaluation, if it is extreme, can make a significant difference to the 'temperature' of the course. If the course 'temperature' gets up to the red (danger) level, the teaching staff receive a 'please explain' letter from their head of school and may be subject to disciplinary action beyond that.

Websites which allow students to randomly comment on staff, whether on the intranet or the Internet are now a global phenomenon. Some of them are on open access, available to anyone around the world, regardless of the reason for their interest or the students' particular motivation for putting comments up.

Of course generic student evaluations of academic staff or courses are not necessarily unfavourable to academics. But whether they are or not, they remain methodologically and ethically problematic such that any results are more or less meaningless. Take, for example, this report from the *Times Higher Education Supplement* (30 January 2004, p. 11) about the pilot of the proposed 'National Student Survey' in the UK. The journalist, Olga Wojtas, writes:

> Findings show that students rate overall quality highly and give the biggest thumbs-up to teaching and improving generic skills, with an average of 3.9 out of a possible 5. Most students feel they have gained confidence in tackling unfamiliar problems and have improved their communication skills. Assessment and learning resources gained 3.7 out of 5. Learning support gained 3.3, and university departments were awarded 3.2 for feedback and workload.

The survey is flawed in a number of ways.

- It gives university teachers no indication whatsoever of how they might improve their teaching.
- All the categories are reduced to generic items such as 'feedback and work load', 'communications skills' and so on, so there is no room to think about specificities.
- While most university courses would be interested in helping students develop their communication skills, this is not likely to be the overarching purpose of all courses (unless it is a vocational course for, say, journalists).

As you can see, academic staff are under surveillance from 'above' (management) and 'below' (students). The demand that they 'improve' their teaching practice has come at exactly the same time as their work loads have intensified drastically. Expansion of student numbers has not been accompanied by matching increases in funding, leading to much larger classes, more marking and so on. The managerialist way of dealing with this problem is to ratchet up the mechanisms for surveillance of academics. Hence they have introduced rules about such things as 'turn-round' time for assessment and phone calls, making yourself available on email and in your office and so on – paying no regard to the fact that having a rule about turn-round time doesn't make it easier to mark 200 essays overnight. Simultaneously, a language of derision about supposedly labour-intensive ways of teaching has emerged and teachers are accused of running courses that are economically not viable. For example, seminar/tutorial teaching is more expensive than lecturing – leading to the reduction in the number of the former in favour of the latter despite good evidence that lectures are a poor vehicle for both teaching and learning.

It is easy to make the observation that managerialists' money is not where their mouths are with regard to the improvement of the quality of university pedagogies. Rather than being put into supporting the teaching that academics do, money is usually diverted into surveillance mechanisms and the employment of staff to support them.

As if this wasn't enough, academic teachers are constantly required to develop 'innovative' approaches to teaching. What is usually meant by this? Interestingly, innovation in teaching is often (if not always) linked with the use of ICTs, and academic staff who make their course materials available on-line are often understood as being 'innovative'. This is the case even when face-to-face practices are simply transferred to virtual worlds. For instance, lecture notes, readings, reading lists and instructions for assignments are placed on the course website. This may be useful, but it is certainly not innovative. It is just another means of handing things out. It may be called 'distributed learning', but it is more about redistributing the costs of materials from the institution to the students than about teaching and learning. Such things are often associated with the notion of 'flexible delivery' and the arguments made in support of this are that students should be able to access the university, their courses and their teachers 24/7 and on demand. In other words, students shouldn't be forced to come to class in order to participate in their university education.

Clearly, it is proper to provide for students who have legitimate reasons – for example, living in remote locations – for not being able to attend campus classes. And it is entirely appropriate that pedagogies are developed which include the use of ICTs to support their learning. However, the danger associated with the notion of 'flexible delivery' is that clicks come to replace bricks, text comes to replace teachers and, overall, the possibilities arise of franchising course materials and is the employment of contract labour to assess students' work. There is a popular fantasy among many people in universities, management and academics alike, that on-line (flexible, virtual, electronic, e-learning or whatever your local language is) teaching is a way of saving effort and money. Anyone who has experience of developing well thought out, pedagogically sound distance learning material knows otherwise – and so do their accountants.

The institutional politics of pedagogy

As we indicated in Chapter 1, this all leaves academics between a rock and hard place. Don't allow such things to put you off teaching, which can be one of the most rewarding parts of academic life. What we'd like to do now is show you some examples of what good university teachers are able to do, in regard to the some of the buzz words we noted earlier.

Key skills

According to the 'quality' vernacular, all university courses must help students develop measurable 'key skills'. These include the ability to make presentations, communicate clearly, solve problems and work in teams – all of them things that many students can already do when they arrive. Certainly these things might underpin the pedagogies of many courses but usually the main focus is on getting students to engage with content and ideas rather than such basic skills.

Ahmed, a junior but highly qualified, much valued academic, is recognised by his students and other staff as a gifted and exceptionally conscientious teacher. He teaches an architecture course with large undergraduate numbers. While he was away on vacation, a senior colleague who regarded herself as a 'quality facilitator' redefined the assessment of Ahmed's course. The new assessment required each student to give a ten-minute talk in class on a subject determined by Ahmed. He was supposed to give each of them a mark and feedback on the presentation skills they exhibited. Ahmed became self-destructively angry and upset about this unwarranted, unjustifiable and high-handed intervention. He went to see his mentor, a senior professor, who became very concerned when Ahmed broke down in tears. His mentor judged that a confrontational response would only make the situation worse. Together they devised an altogether better strategy.

Ahmed already regularly incorporated presentations from students, followed by class discussion, into his teaching. He always insisted that form and content were integrated and included in the class discussion questions of how the form could be improved – developing strict

▶

ground rules with the students about how they should offer their feedback in order to be critically supportive of each other. He decided that, rather than have the students do a whole new set of presentations, as prescribed by the 'quality facilitator', he would give all the students a high mark, provided they gave a reasonable presentation showing evidence of some work.

Doing it this way meant that the only thing he had to change was that the presentations had to be graded.

Was Ahmed's response pedagogically responsible? We think it was. Despite his evident distress and initial panic, he sensibly sought advice from a sympathetic senior colleague. He avoided confrontation and barely changed what he actually had intended to do in the first place.

There are a number of key points (as distinct from key skills) to note here. First, the 'quality facilitator' had no idea how Ahmed actually taught his classes, didn't bother to find out before interfering in the assessment and didn't even consider whether what she was imposing would be an appropriate strategy for this particular course. Second, such pedagogically irresponsible interventions need not necessarily have pedagogically irresponsible responses. Because Ahmed was committed to good teaching he was able to turn a negative into a positive.

Innovation

A dictionary definition of 'innovation' is 'the act or process of inventing or introducing something new' or 'something newly invented or a new way of doing things'. However, universities have tended to adopt the OECD definition of innovation, which is largely associated with creating knowledge that can be commercialised. In teaching, 'innovation' is usually associated with the introduction of ICTs. This widens the potential for the sale of university courses because they are not bounded by physical location.

Faculty at the University of Cleckhuddersfax are under pressure to introduce ICTs in their teaching – or rather, to put all their courses on line. The justification is that it is important for teaching to be innovative

▶ and flexible and, moreover, the university is concerned that when teaching quality is next audited, it will fall down as a result of teaching methods perceived to be old-fashioned. Staff in the fine arts department were well versed in the use of ICTs and were keen to develop multimedia approaches to their teaching and, indeed, to teach the use of multimedia in installation art. Unfortunately the equipment required cost more than the department could afford from its devolved budget, so they used the opportunity to ask their university for additional investment to set up a new multimedia centre for research and teaching. Katie, the head of department, produced a convincing business plan to show management that such a development would become profitable within the medium term and that it would attract international interest and prestige. The university agreed to allocate significant funds to the development of the new centre and the department successfully sought matching funds from industry.

Here we see a department that is already thinking innovatively (in the dictionary definition) and is ahead of the game in terms of the use of ICTs for teaching. The staff were particularly smart in the way in which they responded to the management imperative and took it to its logical conclusion – to the benefit of staff research and student experience alike. Innovation, by definition, can't be standardised, and they were able to demonstrate to management the benefits of genuine innovation. To its credit, management got the point, but the credit goes largely to Katie, who was able to talk the talk required to persuade management. Staff were particularly appreciative of Katie's efforts because it allowed them to develop the innovative use of multimedia in their practice as artists, researchers and teachers.

Benchmarking

Benchmarking is a management tool which usually identifies 'best practice' in equivalent organisations or systems and then requires others to compare themselves with this 'best practice' and to devise strategies for 'continuous improvement' towards the 'benchmark'. Benchmarking can be done within subjects – say cultural studies in several universities – or across subjects – say, cultural studies and mathematics – depending on the criteria employed.

The School of Literary Studies at Downtown University has been instructed by the university management to benchmark against the School of Commerce in the same university. The School of Commerce is understood to exhibit best practice with regard to student numbers, retention, satisfaction, grades and graduate destinations. Literary Studies is required to produce a planning document which explains how they will achieve equivalence and institute continuous improvement. Faculty in Literary Studies meet to discuss these managerial demands and consider how best to respond. They decide to develop a campaign of resistance that utilises their skill in analysis and critique whilst appearing to engage enthusiastically with the exercise. They start by devising a set of questions, all quite difficult for management to answer, about the methodological and technical issues involved. Rather than asking all their questions in one fell swoop, they drip-feed them to management. Then, when management has been almost worn down, they write suggesting that they would love to benchmark against Crosstown University's School of Literary Studies, a department in a very similar university which has a very high reputation for its teaching, student retention and so on.

What they find when they do the benchmarking exercise is what they already knew but management hadn't taken on board – that, because Crosstown deploys its limited funds to employ academic and teaching support staff rather than extra managers and quality assurers, it has the twice the number of academic staff for the same number of students. They also find that all staff members get a considerable amount of staff support in developing and presenting their courses. For instance, all staff were trained by the university in the use of multimedia in teaching. In other words, staff have more time to devote to students because of the lower numbers, and their pedagogies are richer because they've been trained in the use of multimedia. Application numbers are high because Crosstown School of Literary Studies has developed a local and state-wide reputation for its genuinely innovative approach to teaching and the quality of faculty interactions with students. As a consequence, Crosstown can select better students and retain them and they get better jobs after graduating.

Staff at Downtown School of Literary Studies used these bench-marked findings to press management to increase the spend per student and to introduce staff support systems more pedagogically relevant to literary studies itself.

What do we think about the response of Literary Studies at Downtown? The first point to notice is that they were not cowed by the management imperative. Rather than panicking and allowing themselves to be dragooned into compliance, they used their academic skills of asking difficult questions, detailed analysis and critique to ask a series of well honed questions. They had their own views about what best practice was and how it might best be achieved, and they knew through their epistemic community that the faculty at Crosstown had managed to get this just about right. In nominating their own benchmarking comparator, they were able to better identify the conditions that make for 'best practice' pedagogy in their particular discipline and use it to their own advantage.

Contextualised pedagogies

We finish this chapter by giving some examples that we have seen of approaches to teaching that we have found genuinely inspirational. While they do not provide you with a blueprint for your practice, we hope you will find them helpful in thinking creatively about your own teaching. Remember, good and innovative pedagogical practices in some circumstances may be seen as quite basic in others. Innovation in teaching is about developing new ways of improving your pedagogy within your own contexts.

Graínne teaches in a university in a relatively poor country in Europe. At her university students are in class for fifteen to twenty hours a week – that is, almost as long as they were in class at school – and they have virtually no time to read around their subject. One consequence of students' lack of time for reading is that staff feel they need to compensate by spoonfeeding them. Because of various changes in the structure of the degree to make it consistent with EU practice, Graínne found that one of her major courses would receive more credits and consequently more teaching time. After considerable thought, she decided that what the students really needed was not more time in class but carefully structured time in ▶

▶ which they could learn to read and study independently and explore the issues raised in class more deeply. She also instituted a system of learning diaries which had to be handed in at the end of the course together with student assignments.

As a good teacher, Gráinne recognised the problems of a university education which spoonfeeds students. Her pedagogical challenge was how to ensure that students who had no experience of learning independently could and would actually start to do so. One of the difficulties faced by a lot of university teachers is that they imagine that they can take a group of students who have been educated in one way and suddenly introduce them to something new. What they tend to find in such circumstances is quite a bit of student resistance. In this instance, many students actually didn't mind being spoonfed – after all, it required less work from them. So Gráinne's careful strategy involved making the work interesting, giving them a sufficiently structured framework for doing it so that they didn't feel abandoned, and insisting that they recorded their learning processes and practices in their learning diaries.

Colin taught in an education department responsible for the initial education and training of primary and secondary school teachers. His students were mostly from country areas in Australia and tended to be somewhat parochial in their experience and outlook and to have a very short-term view of education. They were particularly concerned about developing their teaching practice and many were quite impatient with courses that insisted on their developing conceptual thinking about pedagogy and schooling. Colin and his teaching team developed a new course on 'Educational Futures'. The team's approach was to get the students to think about futures in terms of social structures, educational inequality and the potential for educational transformation. The taught part of the course focused on the conceptual issues involved. The students' final assignment required them to undertake a case study of an individual pupil whom they identified (and anonymised) from their most recent school-based teaching practice as likely to have a bleak future of social exclusion. They had ▶

▶ to consider both why their case study pupil's future was likely to be bleak in current circumstances and to map out a range of alternative scenarios in which education might play a transformative role, justifying why they thought this could be the case. In doing so, they were required to investigate how comparable social exclusion and inequalities were addressed in a range of other countries and the politics of the different approaches they found.

The team eschewed a conventional approach to the notion of 'futures education', which usually focuses on the implications of information technology for social, cultural and educational change. Rather, it looked at the relationship between futures and social and cultural inequality and challenges to such inequality. It met the students' urgently felt need for practical strategies in their teaching, while insisting that they developed their strategies by engaging conceptually with the course material. Further, it required them to think outside their own immediate geographical location and, in so doing, challenged their parochial views of education.

Jeses teaches a course in the sociology of globalisation. He runs his courses in the conventional lecture/tutorial format and is fortunate that the lecture theatres at his university are particularly well set up for the use of technology. He is able to access his computer desktop from the lecture theatre and go straight to his previously bookmarked favourites on his Web browser. In lectures about the social activism that has arisen around questions of globalisation, he is thus able to go directly to the various activist websites and show them to students on the large screen at the front. He suggests that in their own time they should join in some of the Web conversations, to participate in some of the debates about the effects of globalisation and to share their findings and experiences in tutorials. He also encourages students to identify the impact of globalisation on their own everyday lives. Indeed, one of his tutorial sessions is given over to a street walk during which students identify all the global brands in the street and on selected supermarket shelves.

Jeses has been very concerned about the high levels of abstraction associated with sociological theories of globalisation. He has seen students turned off the topic because they simply can't relate to it – although he, personally, finds it fascinating. Consequently, he has ensured that his course on globalisation helps the students come to grips with its implications for their own lives and the lives of others around the world. Here we have an example of someone who is using ICTs to good effect along with a range of other resources immediately to hand.

And finally ...

It is important to understand that there is no such thing as decontextualised pedagogy. A lot of teaching manuals fall into the trap of thinking that it is possible to develop a one-size-fits-all approach to teaching and learning. As we've indicated throughout this chapter, what is possible and preferable will depend very much on the politics of your own institution and your capacity to deal creatively with such politics. It will also depend on your own ingenuity when it comes to the imperatives of your particular discipline and the students in your classes.

Teaching Identities

In this chapter we attend to some issues that are central to your work as a teacher – developing your teacher identity, building your teaching portfolio and managing your time.

Developing yourself as a teacher

You should aim to plan the development of your experience and profile as a teacher in exactly the same proactive way as you should your research (see *Getting Started on Research*). The list we will shortly give you of what might be included in your teaching portfolio offers some insight, we think, into the sorts of activities you should be undertaking and the experience you should be seeking to acquire. As you compile your portfolio you will be able to identify where the gaps and overlaps are. Try to make sure that you have a balanced portfolio with no major omissions.

Work load

Try to take some reasonable control over the direction that your teaching career is travelling in. With regard to the overall shape of your teaching work load, you should plan your teaching commitments with care and in consultation with your colleagues, mentors and managers. You shouldn't be asked, or offer, to take on too many new courses in a year. When you take a course over, it should be on the understanding that you will keep it for a reasonable period: the start-up costs involved with beginning or taking over a new course can be very high and you need to get some economies of scale. Don't spread yourself too thinly. Teaching on too many courses means that you can't give your proper attention to any of them or to the students on them.

People are often scared of undertaking teaching in new areas. We would not recommend that you develop new courses or take on new teaching in areas in which you have no interest. However, developing new courses can be interesting and exciting for you if you are interested in the field, even if you don't yet have specialist expertise. It is a great way to get into new areas of literature. Having to teach a subject really forces you to make sure that you understand it. In some departments there may be real obstacles to developing new courses. For instance, colleagues anxious to defend their own territory or to defend student numbers enrolled on their own courses. The more universities cut back on staffing, the more vulnerable staff will feel. You have to negotiate your way through this, patiently, carefully and diplomatically, remembering that you don't have a God-given right to teach any course you like regardless of your colleagues' interests or the course's viability. Courses with very small student numbers are costly to run and the university is unlikely to support you in developing them.

Technical skills

Try to make sure that your technical skills are suitably and frequently updated and are what you require. This applies especially to IT, which is a fast moving environment. IT can provide a powerful range of tools that can really make teaching more effective, flexible, interesting and accessible. Conversely, don't be seduced into spending huge amounts of time learning fancy new IT skills that really, when you are honest with yourself, don't actually contribute much to your teaching. We all have colleagues who spend endless hours doing more and more sophisticated PowerPoint presentations with animation and sound effects who actually deliver pretty prosaic and boring lectures that are a triumph of form over content.

The more universities understand their capacity to attract a broader student base as a function of technology, and the more student numbers increase, the more the pressure is on teaching staff to put all their courses on-line and to do more and more on-line teaching. One of the arguments made here is that it is a flexible approach that attends to the needs of students. This may or may not be the case. There are several things to keep in mind under such circumstances, one of which relates to the IT issues mentioned above. However, there are broader peda-gogical questions that you, as a teacher, need to resolve:

- What is best taught on-line and what is not?
- What are the best ways of teaching on-line?
- What technology and what technological competencies do you and your students have and need?

Don't make the mistake of assuming that the pedagogies that you adopt in face-to-face teaching automatically transfer successfully to the on-line environment. Neither should you make the big mistake of thinking that teaching on-line will save you time or effort. It is, in fact, one of the most demanding forms of teaching you can do in both these respects. All that said, it is useful to keep in conversation with those who are at the leading edge in the use of IT in teaching because they will know about the latest software packages that might well enhance your teaching on-line.

In thinking about the relationship between teaching and technology, don't forget that there are a variety of technologies at your disposal. They include such 'old-fashioned' things as the telephone, video, film or audio recordings and the well worn and trusty overhead projector (which is less likely to let you down than your slick PowerPoint presentation).

Training to teach

Increasingly, new academics are required to undertake some formal teacher training. If the course is good, which sometimes they are, you may find it genuinely supportive and helpful. If it is bad, which they sometimes are, you just have to get through it as best you can. If you have a choice as to whether and which course to attend, then do your homework on their quality and choose the one that suits your needs and style.

In the UK, there is government pressure to formalise the training and continuing professional development of university teachers. A national body, the Institute of Learning and Teaching, has been established to accredit university teachers. In order to get the institution going, the initial route to membership for experienced teachers is less rigorous than is usual for any professional accreditation body. This initial route to membership, originally intended to stand for just one year, has now been extended to three years as academics have experienced some inertia when it comes to applying. There has been considerable pressure from university managers to try and make people join. Sometimes they insist that promotion is dependent upon membership of the ILT. Many universities pay individuals' first-year

▶

▶ membership fee. Many of our less experienced colleagues who have been pressured or coerced into joining the ILT have decided, once they have achieved membership, not to renew it. In this way, they have met their university's requirements, while not colluding with a process for managing teachers with which they fundamentally disagree.

Problematic teaching personalities

Be reflexive about your teaching personality and *modus operandi*. There are two extremes in teaching personality types, both of which you need to avoid. At one end of the scale is the teacher who gives no time outside class and has made an art of positively avoiding and shunning students. Their teaching style in the classroom is likely to be one which holds the students at a distance – constantly talking at the students and taking up all the space and time in the class so as to exclude them. This person is being unfair to their colleagues as well as their students because the follow-on effects of their behaviour will impact on their colleagues. This kind of approach puts pressure on more conscientious teachers to pick up the pieces, tutoring neglected students and dealing with their problems and issues. If you are teaching in such circumstances and this burden becomes too great, then you need to talk to your head of department or mentor about it.

At the other extreme is the teacher who not only mothers but also smothers their students. Jane calls this the problem of the 'eternal breast' – succour (sucker) on demand. You are not your students' mother, their therapist or life coach. Not only are these inappropriate roles for you as a teacher (you may do more harm than good if you are giving advice that you are not qualified to offer) but you are also implicitly creating additional burdens for colleagues by creating unduly high expectations about what staff will do. If you hand out your home phone number to undergraduates, are constantly at their beck and call, read endless drafts of their assignments and generally exceed the boundaries of your real responsibilities, then you create the impression that all your colleagues will do the same. This is an unfair imposition on them. You and your colleagues should mutually agree on the service levels that you give to students and then stick to them except in very unusual circumstances.

If you are a mothering/smothering teacher you really need to look deep inside yourself and decide whether you are doing it because you think it is good teaching practice or because, for your own reasons, you have some real need to be loved and wanted. Playing out such desires has no place in good teaching. That's not to say, however, that you can't and shouldn't get a real kick out of students admiring and respecting you, or even loving you, but you need to keep a balance between necessary availability and care and keeping appropriate boundaries.

One almost parental point from us. Do not, on any account, ever and for any reason become sexually, emotionally or romantically involved with any of your students. We have said enough about the power relations present in the pedagogic relationship to make it self-evident why this is fundamentally abusive. It is generally a good idea to stay well away, in this sense, from *all* students in your university. Personal relationships of this sort are inevitably complicated and, if you must jump into these troubled waters, you need to think very carefully and very deeply before doing so. Furthermore, you must declare your interest with regard to such students in any situation where you may have some influence or be privy to any confidential material about their studies. For instance, you might be on a committee considering their grades or degree classification, and this is clearly problematic.

Building your teaching portfolio

What do you mean by a teaching portfolio?

It is a personal professional record of your teaching that can be used in various ways – as a resource for your teaching and as a record for such things as promotion. Your first year of teaching in higher education in a substantive post, regardless of your previous teaching experience or expertise in the field, is likely to be the single most exhausting and enervating year in your entire career. Everyone goes through it and the good news is that it does get better. There are two reasons why the first year is so hard. One is that you haven't learned the smart tricks that let you get by more easily. More important is that you have little or nothing in your personal teaching bank to call on. You will probably be dealing with new courses and possibly unfamiliar material.

As a resource

Your teaching portfolio provides you with ready access to past work and acts as a sort of teaching savings account on which you can draw (though, unlike your bank account, it won't become depleted when you call on it). So you will want to deposit all the materials that you think will be of future use to you in your teaching portfolio. These teaching banks are also resources that you can share with colleagues and they can share theirs with you. This stops everyone constantly reinventing the wheel, although, of course, you can't abrogate your responsibility to engage directly with and think about your own teaching. You can't pick up and run with someone else's ready-made courses and expect them to work well, notwithstanding the exponential growth in the franchising of teaching materials and courses. You may be in a position in which you are not developing the course on which you teach – for example because you are a graduate teaching assistant, a casually employed teacher or a tutor on a distance learning course such as those run by the UK's Open University. Clearly you have significantly less autonomy in these circumstances and you are unlikely to be free to decide what you teach. You will, however, be able to plan your teaching methods and approaches. The course materials and these plans can all go into your portfolio.

In building your portfolio, you need to keep in mind that universities are now marketised institutions that commodify knowledge. This means that the intellectual products of university staff, such as teaching materials, are increasingly being placed formally and legally under the control of institutions. That is, universities may seek to assert intellectual property rights over your teaching materials. Where this assertion of rights occurs, it seeks to supplant existing collegial systems where professionals shared their materials. For some universities, control over intellectual property is important because they make serious money out of selling courses and franchising them. Your legal situation will vary according to your contract of employment and the law of the country where you are working. You should properly inform yourself about your own situation with regard to IPR on teaching materials. This is particularly problematic for materials that you might place on the intra- or Internet such as lecture notes. Bear in mind that anything to which you give a public material or electronic form may become the university's property. There are two competing traditions at work here. One is that of colleagues sharing teaching materials and acknowledging their provenance. The other is the claim that employers own these materials and can prevent academic staff from freely exchanging materials. Again, we see an example of the ways in which the marketised university can undermine academic freedom and modes of collegiality which enhance teaching.

In *Getting Started on Research* you will find extensive guidance on writing research proposals. This began life when Debbie wrote some shorter guidelines for her master's students at the Institute of Education. Debbie agreed to allow it to be reproduced for a wider student audience. She then shared it with Rebecca, who developed it further and used it in her own masters teaching and then placed it on her university's website to help applicants for doctoral places. Debbie, Rebecca and Jane then used this material in *Getting Started on Research*. The intellectual property rights in that book are shared by us with the publishers. Who has the intellectual property rights in this material?

Interestingly, the material was reproduced at the Institute with no attribution to Debbie. At the University of the West of England, Rebecca claimed the copyright on our behalf. Her university queried it and she insisted that the material could not go on the Web without attribution of copyright to us.

As a record

A further use for your teaching portfolio is that it provides a comprehensive record of your professional teaching practice that you can use for things such as: staff appraisal/performance reviews; promotion applications; tenure applications; and when seeking a new post. You will also find it useful if you need to get your teaching expertise formally accredited.

In assessing your record of teaching achievement, those judging you will be looking at the following sorts of things:

- Good teaching involves the development of original and interesting ideas both for content and for pedagogy. You need to show that you can think not only about what you teach, but also about how you teach. These ideas will have to be appropriate to the material, your disciplinary area and the students involved.

- One of the things that every competent teacher in higher education should be able to do is to create and mount courses in particular areas, on particular subjects, at various levels.
- As your teaching career progresses, you should be able to demonstrate that you can put together whole degree programmes that have coherence, intellectual integrity and also appeal to students.
- Again, as your teaching career develops, you will be expected to have taught successfully across the complete range of students, from first-year undergraduates to doctoral research students.
- Courses and degree programmes occur within distinct institutional structures and are framed by regulations and university procedures. You must be able to show that you can go further than the drawing board, taking your ideas for teaching, fashioning them and steering them through formal procedures to the point where they become actual programmes.

Alarmed at the lack of deep intellectual thinking among their masters students, Robert and Andreas designed a reading-based course in which they tried to get the students to engage with the great classical texts in their discipline from the previous fifty years. When they took their proposed course to the relevant university committee for approval, the outline reading list, which they had been required to include, was severely and roundly criticised by managers because it was 'out of date'. Rather than fight people who clearly did not understand the rationale of the course, they simply removed the older of their chosen classic texts from the official documentation and resubmitted it. The course was duly approved. In the documentation that went to the students (and in Andreas and Robert's teaching portfolios) they reinstated all the original texts.

- As a professional teacher in higher education, you should be able to work with others in teams to develop and teach courses. You will need evidence of this in your portfolio.
- Good academics see teaching and research as a seamless web. There is a synergy between teaching and research at both first and higher

degree levels. In order to do good research, you will, inevitably, be engaged with and fascinated by your subject. This will enable you to teach it with enthusiasm. You must be able to demonstrate that you have translated your research-led engagement with your subject into your teaching.

- You need to be able to show that the students you have taught feel that they have, for most part, derived enjoyment and benefit from your teaching even if, at times, they found the work difficult, confusing or challenging. In fact, when they find the work challenging, realise there are no right answers and are moved to work hard to try to make sense of things, then you are doing a really good job.

- Finally, the proof of the educational pudding is whether your students generally make satisfactory progress. In managerialist terms, progress means their relative success in passing assessments. However, we think other forms of progress are equally important. These include things like: helping students who might otherwise drop out to stay with the course; assisting all students to achieve their own objectives, even if these don't have much institutional cachet; or making sure that all or most of your students know how to learn for themselves.

What to include in your teaching portfolio

Here is a reasonably comprehensive list. We suggest that these should be on your computer, backed up on disk and also in hard copy. Clearly your teaching portfolio will also include a number of artefacts that can't be kept on your computer.

- *Course outlines*, especially for courses you develop yourself or with others. Keep both the documentation submitted to the university for approval and the stuff that the students actually receive. The official documentation may be useful to you in future if and when you need to go through similar exercises. The documentation for students will demonstrate much better your approach to teaching and your engagement with them.

- *Lesson plans, teaching/lecture notes, overhead projector slides or PowerPoint presentations.* Don't forget to include any agendas or other hand-outs that you have prepared for students.

- Related to your lesson plans will be *activity sheets, games, exercises, teaching aids,* and *seminar notes* for colleagues who teach on your courses, particularly when they are innovative and exciting. Increasingly, university teachers are expected to demonstrate that their programmes are innovative, especially when applying for a new job. As noted earlier, 'innovative teaching' is not synonymous with using digital technologies in teaching, though it may include it. It may also include opening up teaching in new subject areas, developing new teaching methods and/or materials, attracting a new body of students, forging new interdisciplinary links in your teaching.
- *Examples of materials produced by others that you have used.* These will include videos/DVDs, audio material, artefacts, visual images, newspaper cuttings and so on. You will need a note to yourself about how you used them and in what contexts.
- *Student evaluations and other kinds of feedback.* This will vary from formal student evaluation questionnaires that your department or university may insist on (summative assessments) to nice letters from students in which they talk about the impact of your teaching on them. If you are in a position in which you must use the evaluation questionnaires designed by others for management purposes, it is a good idea also to get students to give you additional, formative, feedback in a more useful way for developing your teaching.

Shannon allocates time for students to discuss with her how they feel the course is progressing and makes iterative adjustments in the light of their feedback. In addition to this oral feedback, she asks students at the end of the course to reply in writing to the following three questions:

- What did you enjoy about the course?
- What constructive suggestions can you make for improving it next year?
- Do you have any other comments about the course?

This formative feedback helps her to shape her subsequent teaching.

At the end of each course you should be able to write a short reflection on your own teaching and put it alongside your students' evaluations to contextualise what the students have said. This is particularly important if you feel that the evaluations don't really reflect what went on in the course.

Often generic university questionnaires are not appropriate for your teaching, your students or your courses. Another disadvantage of such generic feedback forms is that they permit, even encourage, the occasional abusive act by individual students even in the best taught classes and at the best universities. You should not feel obliged to retain, or pass on to anyone else, feedback that is personally abusive or patently troublemaking. You should be aware that it is common for people in certain groups to have had, at least once, anonymous racist, homophobic and/or sexist comments and for all staff to have had adverse comments about their personal appearance, dress sense and so on. The best thing to do with such feedback, if you can't identify the perpetrator, is to treat it with the contempt it deserves. You should also bring such incidents to the attention of the appropriate university authorities. Even if such material does not particularly upset you, other colleagues may be distressed by it, and reporting it may lead to the whole issue being addressed.

- You may have to produce formal *written reports* on your course either for 'quality assurance' purposes or to act as guidance to external examiners or validation bodies. When you are writing such reports, do bear in mind that they have an extremely public audience. Be honest, but be very careful in your phraseology, as bad wording can come back to haunt you. This is not the place for teaching confessions. Everyone screws up from time to time, and you may need to discuss this with a supportive colleague, but you definitely do not need it on the university's official records.
- Your university may have formal mechanisms, such as *course committees or staff–student liaison committees*, where student representatives can give formal feedback on teaching and raise any issues of concern. Minutes of these may be included in your portfolio.

- Examples of the formative *feedback* you give students on their work indicate the quality of your engagement with them. They need to be written to reflect the respect that you show your students in your teaching. Remember that students need a balance of comments that affirm their work and those that suggest ways of improving it.
- Keep a good record of any work of an *administrative nature* related to teaching that you have undertaken. You may have been the director of a degree programme, chair of a student progression committee, responsible for collecting and collating examination marks in your department and so on. Demonstrating that you have done such work and done it well will enable you to show that you are a good colleague and also have a keen understanding of university processes and procedures with regard to teaching.
- University teaching now frequently involves staff in team teaching efforts on specific courses. You might be working with a group of peers or be responsible for co-ordinating the efforts of any number of sessional teachers or Teaching Assistants. Do not underestimate the skills required for this sort of team working and teaching leadership. Keep good records of where you have worked in this way to show that you can and will do it.
- If you have helped and mentored less experienced colleagues in their teaching, it is useful to keep a record of this, in the form of either your own notes or copies of theirs (with their permission).
- If you become known to be a good 'performer' as a teacher, you may well receive invitations to offer specialist classes, or even entire courses, in other departments, faculties or even universities. Keeping records of such work is a marker of the esteem in which your colleagues elsewhere hold you. Similarly, if your course materials are used by other colleagues, either at your institution or elsewhere, keep a note of it.
- If you know that your publications are used in teaching at other institutions, it's useful to have a record of it, for example by getting a copy of the relevant course outlines.
- The more senior you become the more you will be expected to demonstrate not only that you have taught but that you have successful experience of teaching leadership. This may include managing teams of seminar leaders, developing new programmes and courses, introducing new ideas into your courses, leading collaborative teams and managing all the administrative aspects of running large course or degree programmes.

What your mother never told you about time

Everyone we know who works in a university is chronically short of time. Here are some issues to think about in relation to your own time.

Don't forget research. Teaching is, for the most part, a highly structured and formal activity. Apart from one-to-one supervision, tutorials and some aspects of on line teaching you will have to be in a set place, at a set time, with a particular group of students over a particular period. This gives a largely non-discretionary structure to your working week for a significant proportion of the year. This means that you can't ignore teaching and put it on the back burner in the same way that you might do with your research. As such, it's important that you always keep the fact that you have other things to do, such as research, in the foreground of your thoughts and planning. Don't let the formal, compulsory nature of teaching duties swamp out all the other stuff that you must do. This may feel more discretionary because it doesn't occur at fixed times, but it is not.

Busy work and necessary admin. The other activity that has some sort of formal imperative is administration. If you don't submit your exam questions in the appropriate form at the appropriate time, for example, it can cause real problems for all concerned. That said, you need to distinguish carefully between those aspects of the administration of teaching that are truly necessary and important and those which are nothing more than time-wasting trivia. We told you the story earlier on of Boubacar and Achille and their reaction to such 'busy work' (see also *Getting Started on Research*).

Balance your work activities. You may work in a department that has some sort of formal system for the allocation of time between activities such as research and teaching. Some systems just allocate teaching time and expect staff to get on with their research in the time remaining. If you have such a system, try to use it to make sure that you are spending an appropriate proportion of your annual working time on each of teaching, research and administration. You can use these schemes in arguments about work as a justificatory device to make sure that you are not pressured or guilt-tripped into spending undue time on teaching and/or admin.

Timetabling and 'joined up' time. Because you need 'joined up', connected periods of time to get on with your research, it is imperative that your periods of teaching are not spread, like confetti, across the entire week. Timetabling is a real skill and you and your colleagues should work hard with your timetabler to make sure that she or he knows what your needs are. Resist any managerialist system that always prioritises expediency and the needs of 'students as customers'. At an individual level, do your best, when organising your own courses, classes and lectures, to make sure that you protect important research time while still behaving ethically towards students and recognising their legitimate needs. Be a good colleague and, when making teaching arrangements that involve others, bear in mind that your co-workers also need consideration.

Fatu, a lecturer of some years' standing, was struggling to find enough time to complete her doctoral thesis. She taught a second-year undergraduate course and her more senior colleague, Lindsay, taught a related third-year course. Lindsay suggested, for good pedagogical reasons, that they should take some of the seminar groups on each other's courses so that they could develop and maintain better continuity between their two courses for the benefit of the students. The trouble was that all the seminar classes on Lindsay's course were held on the only day of the week that Fatu had otherwise free of teaching and on which she liked to stay at home and work on her thesis. She discussed this with her mentor, who suggested that she explain the problem to Lindsay. Lindsay was very understanding and they agreed to defer their planned swap to the following year, when they could make more mutually satisfactory timetabling arrangements.

It is obviously helpful to be able to get all your teaching on to two or three days in the week if you possibly can. Another good strategy, if you can manage it, is to try to get the bulk of your teaching duties concentrated in one term or semester. We often imagine managing an academic work load as a bit like the old-fashioned circus act, where the performer sets dinner plates spinning on top of poles, the art being to keep as many of them spinning at the same time as possible without letting them crash to the ground. The entertainment value lies in watching the increasingly frantic activity of the performer as they race around maintaining each plate's momentum. This may be entertaining for circus audiences, but it's not much fun as a working life for academics. If you can divide your working year such that you have very concentrated periods of one activity such as teaching, followed by another such as research, you will be far more productive and far less exhausted.

Miranda was head of a nurse education programme in a university health sciences faculty that was placing increasing stress on research. The programme as it stood involved having both university-based teaching and hospital practice taking place across the whole year. Thus there were always some students needing lectures, seminars and tutorials and others needing to be supervised on their placements. This meant that members of the teaching team had virtually no discretionary time in which they could do their research.

Miranda led her team in a reorganisation of the programme, which meant that the university-based teaching for all students was concentrated into the first semester, while clinical work in hospitals was moved into the second. In the new system, the first semester is very intensive and lecturers have very little time. However, in the second they are able to arrange their own timetables for visiting students in order to give themselves connected, joined-up time to do research. A further advantage is that much of the clinical supervision of students is done by experienced staff in the teaching hospital. This relieves academic staff of their commitments and provides them with much more flexibility.

Research days or research daze. We often find it wryly amusing, when we have been rushing round at our universities all day, teaching, seeing students, going to meetings and dealing with our email, that we get home and say, 'I haven't been able to get any work done today.' Of course, this is ironic. What we really mean is that we haven't had the opportunity to do any sustained intellectual work such as reading, writing or thinking about research or teaching. It's very naughty of us to see all the stuff that we do when we are rushing around in our departments as 'not work'. This is one of the many forms of self-flagellation that academics impose on themselves. Because meetings, seeing students and dealing with routine administrative tasks eat into time, it's best to try to get all that stuff done in the interstices of formal classes. This will leave you free on the days when you are not teaching to stay at home and do some 'real work' uninterrupted. On such days, do not on any account be seduced into 'popping in' to work for anything. It will always take up a good part of the day, if not the whole day. Give your apologies for any meetings on your research days and do not be frightened to prioritise research over meetings. Let it be known what your research days are and make clear to your colleagues that you will not be available for anything on those days under any circumstances. Eventually people get the message. Put your answering machine on and turn your email off.

Teaching, learning and pedagogic praxis. We notice that novice teachers tend to replicate the teaching practices by which they were taught. Practice makes practice, as the Canadian academic, Deborah Britzman, says. And, as Gramsci would say, 'history has congealed into habit' here. It is better pedagogically and in your own best interests to design your teaching (as distinct from scheduling it) in such a way that students quickly become accustomed to taking responsibility for their own learning. For example, if you are teaching students how to do a literature search, consider setting them a group exercise that they have to undertake independently in the library rather than you standing and doing a 'chalk and talk' act. You can always check how well the students have done on the exercise by getting them to do a short presentation back to the class. Many institutions have 'mission statements' and suchlike that espouse the virtues of 'independent learning' and 'student empowerment'. We are inclined to be cynical about such statements, often seeing them as weasel words and managerialist-speak, combined as they usually are with reductionist notions which direct teachers to adopt easily defined 'learning outcomes' and the 'objective measurement' of education. However, when students take real responsibility for their own learning processes, they invariably find it the most educationally satisfying experience that they can have. Equally, as a teacher, it is very rewarding to see students develop in this way.

You should be aware, however, that this kind of teaching does have heavier than usual start-up costs and requires careful preparation.

Students have to be trained and inducted into that sort of approach, especially if they are used to being spoonfed with predigested gobbets of pap-like information. Some students will need additional support to help them adjust to these methods. However, done well, this becomes low-maintenance, low-cost and satisfying teaching.

> Wu was a senior academic in the UK who had strong research links in Australia. During a busy teaching term he needed to go to Australia to pursue his research interests. He spent a few weeks training his seminar students to run their own classes. He equipped them with topics, suitable materials and discussed with them what they would like to achieve. He then went to Australia and let them get on with it on their own. The students in Wu's department regularly voted for a 'Teacher of the Term'. Wu won this accolade during the term in which he ran this experiment and went away. This wasn't an ironic statement by the students (although we tease him that it was); it was just that the students found the whole experience immensely enjoyable and it made them feel as if they were being treated as the mature, responsible people they in fact were.

Some forms of teaching, such as formal lectures, are much more labour-intensive than others. Additionally, many of these types of teaching are actually quite ineffective but tend to be popular with unconfident teachers and lazy students. They therefore have little to recommend them either as a pedagogical device or as a way of getting your work load under control. We say more about lectures below in the section on developing your teaching.

Working at social time. A lot of academic work is quite isolated and lonely. It's a good idea to try, as far as you can, to make busy time at work also act as pleasant social time. You might, for instance, take a lunch or coffee break with colleagues in your own or other departments. A lot of academics we know, including ourselves sometimes, tend to eat a sandwich at our desks. This is really not a good idea – either for your digestion or for your mental well-being. It's better to make a point of going to the coffee bar, canteen or wherever people tend to congregate. That way you get some social interaction and, very often, hear the important gossip, network and actually get some university work done in the process.

Some of the best teaching and research ideas start and are developed over a cup of coffee (or even herbal tea) or lunch. Where small meetings are not confidential, formal or difficult, it's often a good idea to go and have a coffee (or whatever) with the colleagues or students involved. We have had many a productive research meeting or supervision over just such coffee tables – and they can also be the best places to sort out departmental problems (provided you don't need confidentiality). Remember that such social time is not time wasted.

Email is a really important means of communication with colleagues and students all over the world. However, it can also invade your day, fragmenting your time and distracting you from getting on with more substantial tasks. This problem is acute in all walks of professional and commercial life. It is also treacherously easy to think that you must answer an email immediately, without really considering what your answer should be. It is possible to tame this beast. Consider strategies such as opening your email only at a set time each day. On days when you are working at home, consider not looking at your email at all. Pick low value/low energy times to deal with your email correspondence – but if you have an important email to write, don't do it then. Consider having a separate email address for important research projects, significant correspondents or for your personal email.

And finally ...

It's worth pointing out that a teacher identity is something that is built. It comes with time, work and experience. In difficult times, many teachers are tempted to become cynical and jaded in relation to the work. This is understandable but not at all helpful in developing creative strategies for making your teaching a rewarding activity in itself. One of the most satisfying things about being a teacher is the opportunity it provides for you to make a major difference to people's lives. The saying 'everyone remembers a good teacher' has been deployed in advertising campaigns in the UK to recruit schoolteachers, but that does not detract from the fact that it is true. For the jaded and cynical, it is worth remembering that the converse may also be true – few of us forget our really terrible teachers.

In this chapter we have discussed the things you will have to cope with as a teacher and provided you with some advice about how to manage and develop yourself as a teacher. We next consider the teaching associated with postgraduate research students.

5   Postgraduate Research Supervision (I) Getting Going

In this chapter we turn from our focus on undergraduate teaching to consider the supervision of postgraduate research. The chapter starts with a brief discussion of different kinds of postgraduate research programmes. We then turn to the structuring of students' postgraduate research, focusing particularly on PhDs. The second part of the chapter is about your first steps towards becoming a good research supervisor.

What kinds of postgraduate research are there?

At an appropriate point in your academic career, you should begin to take responsibility for the supervision of the research element of postgraduate students' work. These include students doing:

- A research dissertation as part of a taught masters.
- A masters degree by research (often called an MPhil).
- A 'professional' doctorate – these are programmes designed for senior professionals who wish to acquire research skills and a deeper understanding of their professions. Examples include the Doctor of Business Administration (DBA), Doctor of Education (EdD), Doctor of Psychology of Education (DPsychEd).
- A traditional research doctorate (usually called a PhD, but also known as a DPhil or a DLitt).

All these types of programmes will require students to undertake some piece – larger or smaller – of original research.

Like any sort academic work, you need to acquire and develop the skills necessary for this over a period of time. You should not be thrown in at the deep end in an unsupported environment. Nobody should expect you to simply 'know' how to supervise research students, even if you have been one yourself. We all have substantial experience in this area, but are acutely aware that we still need to carry on learning about and reflecting on our supervisory practice. In the rest of this book we offer guidance to those new to supervisory work and those who are more experienced but who are keen to improve their skill.

Of all these different kinds of postgraduate research, the traditional research doctorate (which, for shorthand, we will refer to as a 'PhD') is the most sustained and demanding for student and teacher, and requires considerable skill and experience from the supervisor (who is usually called the 'advisor' in the USA). However, all of them require similar generic skills and processes. Throughout this part of the book we will concentrate on PhD research students, as you will be able to adjust what you do for other kinds of postgraduate research supervision.

The sorts of supervisory experience that can be useful as a precursor to supervising PhD students' theses are:

- Undergraduate research projects or dissertations.
- Masters students' dissertations.
- Shorter research papers undertaken by students on doctoral programmes with a taught element.

Of course, most people undertaking supervisory work are likely to have been supervised themselves at some point in the past and you can learn both good and bad practices from that. Unfortunately, not all supervisors do a good job. Even more unfortunately, some of those who survive such bad practice go on to reproduce it themselves when they become supervisors. Drawing on Alice Miller, we call this 'Poisonous Pedagogies of Supervision'.

Why ask students to do research?

We think that there are a number of reasons why degree programmes include greater or lesser elements of research by students:

- Research encourages independent thinking and the development of students' intellectual creativity.
- It provides an opportunity for students to pursue their own interests in a close way.

- Undertaking research develops and tests important practical skills of enquiry, analysis, the application of theory to practice and problem solving.
- Doing a piece of research tests the student's understanding of their disciplinary field at a deep level.
- High-level research degrees such as PhDs provide training for people to undertake research careers inside or outside the academy. Indeed we would argue that this is one of the most valuable aspects.
- Students usually gain immense personal enjoyment and fulfilment from completing such a piece of work, even if they find it very hard actually doing it.
- It is the ultimate educational form: it's about knowledge acquisition and building driven by personal curiosity and requires challenging and difficult work over a sustained period. Ultimately, it should make the student think about some aspect of the world in a very different way.

Karina was a part-time taught master's student studying accountancy. She had no first degree. She is a professional accountant and also the treasurer of the local branch of the political party of which she is a member. When she started her 20,000 word dissertation she envisaged it being a technical description of the effects of new legislation governing the reporting of political parties' income. What she eventually ended up with was a significant, and potentially publishable, theoretical analysis of the relationship between democracy, political marketing and sleaze and how these impact on regulatory controls over political parties. She came to view her own role as treasurer somewhat differently and more reflexively and is now able to make a real contribution to deeper understanding of these issues within her party. Finally, she plans to contribute to wider national debates on this subject using the insights she has gained from her research.

Should students' research be a structured process?

Of course students' research should be structured for them. It is unlikely that students will start their research already equipped with sufficient research skills to enable them to complete the work. Furthermore, an unstructured environment in which students do not get adequate guidance and support is likely to have adverse outcomes. These may include some or all of the following:

- They never finish, or take an eternity to do so. The longest we have ever heard of is sixteen years to complete a PhD that should have taken no more than five. Failure to complete, or delays in completion, are bad for students' self-esteem, job prospects and family life. Failures and delays are also bad for the reputation of the institution.
- Students go off pursuing red herrings down blind alleys (to mix a metaphor or two). This is dispiriting and causes delays and frustration. That said, we think that some element of getting lost and finding your own way back is an integral part of the early stages of a PhD.
- There may be unintended and unfortunate ethical consequences for research respondents and others. These problems can be irreparable, or only fixable with immense institutional effort and expense.
- Students may be ill prepared to deal with physical and emotional dangers, putting them at risk.
- The work fails to reach the expected standard and the student fails the degree entirely or is awarded a lesser qualification.
- Disgruntled students justifiably feel let down by their institution and may even sue.

Institutions have become increasingly aware of these adverse outcomes. Unfortunately, this awareness has been prompted less by the poor quality of student experience than by an assessment of the risks of litigation and also an increase in external regulation and quality assurance monitoring.

Whatever the motivations, we welcome recent efforts to ensure that students are properly supervised and advised throughout their research degrees. For the most part, the enhanced regulatory environment that is developing in many countries is to the students' benefit (unlike the quality audit of other teaching). We think that the reason is that, thus far, the increased regulation of research degrees has been under academic control and has not (yet) become the subject of managerialist interference to any significant extent.

In the UK, the Quality Assurance Agency (QAA), which was set up by the Higher Education Funding Council to monitor and audit teaching quality in universities, is seeking to regulate PhDs. Initially it tried to apply to research degrees its credit rating system for taught degrees (under which the amount of study necessary to achieve a particular degree is determined by reference to the accumulation of a set number of 'credit points' attached to individual courses). It was hoist by its own petard: the credit rating of taught courses is supposedly 'objectively' determined by their individual 'Learning Outcomes'. 'Learning Outcomes' are defined by the QAA as 'objective and measurable' statements of the knowledge, skills and information to be acquired by the student. Of course, by their very nature, research degrees are not amenable to the setting of such narrowly defined 'Learning Outcomes'. The real learning outcomes, in contrast to those defined by bureaucratic regimes, cannot be reduced to narrowly defined and reliably measurable definitions of knowledge, skills and information. Consequently, PhD students will not have to pass x credits at D level (though those doing professional doctorates will).

How are PhDs structured?

The traditional European PhD, a model widely adopted across the world, has had an extremely *laissez-faire* structure. Many people's experience of their own PhD is of being largely left on their own to get on with it in a relatively unstructured way. They muddle through, but many students left to fend for themselves either fail to finish their thesis or complete it on time.

The North American system has traditionally been shaped differently, with considerably more structure and formal interim examination/ assessment of students' progress. North American PhDs also have longer registration periods than their counterparts in, for instance, the UK and Australia. These long registration periods may contribute to fairly significant student drop-out rates. We describe Rohana's experience of doing a PhD in history at an Ivy League university in the USA in Table 1. Although the process described is something of a Rolls-Royce version, we think that the various formal stages that Rohana had to go through illustrate well the actual stages of work that all students should pass

TABLE 1 Time line for a research degree at an Ivy League university in the USA

Time line	Activities	Assessment
Application process	Satisfactory results on Graduate Standard Achievement Tests (GSATS) Application with outline research area and CV	Accepted by university and offered bursary
Year 1	Substantive taught courses in history, historiography (historical method), epistemology and individual reading course(s)	Assessed by course work and presentations MA awarded
Year 2	Substantive taught courses in history, historiography, epistemology, individual reading course(s) and the writing of assessed research papers	Assessed by course work
Year 3	Reading in one major and two minor fields (approximately 100 texts in the major field and fifty in each of the minor fields, chosen by the student in consultation with advisers (supervisors) Preparation of thesis prospectus (i.e. a very detailed and worked through proposal)	Oral examination and grading on reading by advisers (supervisors) Must be judged acceptable by advisers (supervisors). Student is now informally known as 'ABD' – All But the Dissertation.
Years 4–6	Data collection in archives and writing of the doctoral dissertation (thesis)	Read and graded by advisers (supervisors) and PhD awarded. No formal or oral examination

through. In most universities around the world, however, students have to go through these stages without – or with very much less – formal structure. The support that is built into the various courses that Rohana did in the first two years has to be provided by the supervisor, through research education (training) and attendance at appropriate substantive courses, possibly at master's level.

Recent developments in some countries, including the UK, represent a move towards the US-type system, albeit significantly adapted. These changes fall into two types. First, the research training received by students has been formalised and extended. In the social sciences now many universities offer specialist research training masters degrees, taken before the PhD is formally commenced. You can see how this is similar to Rohana's experience in the USA. Second, the specific milestones that students must pass during their doctoral studies are generally taken much more seriously. In addition, the formal reporting and monitoring of student progress have been significantly increased.

When Rebecca first registered as a research student she was enrolled, like all her fellow students, on the MPhil programme. After a year she was allowed to 'upgrade' to the PhD programme. The formal hurdle for this to happen consisted of nothing more than giving a satisfactory departmental seminar to fellow students and some staff. Many years later, as the director of research degrees at a large business school, she oversaw the introduction of a system of progression examination for doctoral students. All intending doctoral students are registered on the PhD programme but within twelve months of first registering (eighteen if they are part-time) the student has to submit a progression report which is subject to formal oral examination by staff other than their supervisors. The progression report has two parts. The first, 6,000 word, part is a detailed synopsis of the intended thesis, together with an account of work done so far and a reflection of any research training the student has had. The second part generally consists of 10,000 words of substantive writing towards the thesis. Alternatively, if the student has done the university's research training masters, their dissertation from that degree is required to be a pilot or feasibility study for the intended doctoral research. In that case, they can submit that dissertation.

In general, we give a cautious welcome to these changes. They offer the prospect of giving students a more carefully structured and guided experience, helping to make sure that they finish, and finish on time and successfully. As we have said before, the submission of the final thesis can feel like an insurmountable hurdle for students in the early (and sometimes in the later) stages. Instituting some sort of structured guidance and interim milestones can help to make the process much more manageable and less daunting for all concerned. Formal requirements can also be used as a real spur to motivate recalcitrant students.

Should I find the prospect of supervision worrying?

Why might academics be worried about the prospect of supervising research students? We think it is very understandable. The causes of anxiety are likely to include at least some of the following issues:

- Whilst student research has a number of common characteristics, students are likely to be engaged in a bewildering variety of degree programmes with a whole host of different expectations. Understanding the nuanced differences between the standards and expectations of different research degree programmes can be a complex task and something that calls for real professional judgement.
- Failure to do this work well can have serious consequences for the student and, sometimes, for the institution. If a student fails to get a PhD because of your poor supervision, you have significantly damaged their lives. Supervision is a very big responsibility and not one to be undertaken lightly.
- There is an increasingly stringent regulatory framework in most universities that can be hard to get your head round. Because your student numbers tend to be low, you don't get to learn the rules and regulations by constantly having to apply them.
- It can be very anxiety-inducing, especially at doctoral level, if you feel that you are not *the* expert in the student's intended area of research. The supervisor needs to have sufficient expertise in the area to get the student well underway with the work and to recognise blind alleys. However, you should expect that the student will eventually become more expert than the supervisor. Supervisors can often be more helpful on matters of process than of content.
- We've already noted that training for teaching in higher education can leave a lot to be desired. This is even more the case in training for research supervision. Very many, perhaps most, supervisors have never received any formal supervision training. Consequently they may base their own supervisory practices on their own experience as research students, whether good or bad. In good doctoral

programmes, novice supervisors normally serve a kind of apprenticeship with someone more experienced. They join a team of supervisors in the hope and expectation that they will learn on the job. Sometimes experienced and successful supervisors will work with a student who is researching a topic some way away from their own expertise, in order to provide the support for a less experienced supervisor who is an expert in the field.

Sounds awful – why should I do it?

Despite these common anxieties, we still believe that supervising research students at all levels is just about the best sort of teaching that you can do, ever. We have several reasons for our enthusiasm:

- You can develop wonderful research relationships with students. Their efforts inform your own, feed into your thinking and working, give you new things to think about, engage you with new literatures and so on. Their enthusiasm can be very uplifting when you are coping with a stressful job. At its best, seeing your research students is a highlight in a busy day.
- Because of the intense efforts involved, you can get real pleasure from sharing the students' sense of achievement and satisfaction.
- As you build a body of research students around you, you are helping to develop a whole network of research collaborators and friends who should stay with you for the rest of your career. Thus supervisory work helps to build academic communities and networks in a really organic way.
- You can also significantly further the wider research in your particular field, building your discipline and helping to carve out new areas. You can develop a sense of joint academic endeavour with a good group of students.
- Demonstrating that you are a successful supervisor will enhance your career and promotion prospects.

Am I suitably qualified for this work?

The first thing to ask yourself when contemplating starting to supervise, or if you are currently supervising research at any postgraduate level is, 'Am I suitably qualified to do this work?' No-one should supervise research students if they are not themselves an established and active researcher. By this we mean that you should not supervise postgraduate research unless you yourself have seen at least one substantial project through from conception to completion, including producing academic publications. If you can't or don't do research yourself you simply will not be able to guide others through what is a complex, difficult and highly skilled process.

In addition to being an experienced researcher, we think that you should also be a competent and confident teacher before you take on supervision. This is because being such a teacher will mean that you have the insights necessary to understand how people learn, study and construct knowledge. You will also know something about how to help them understand and write about complex ideas. Ideally, then, supervisory work should be a later developmental stage of your career as a teacher.

If you are an experienced researcher and teacher, then, in our view, you are basically qualified to undertake postgraduate research supervision. If you are already supervising and you do not meet these basic prerequisites, then you should think hard about whether you and your department are acting responsibly towards your student(s).

There are some additional prerequisites. First of all, you should see doctoral supervision as a natural progression from supervising master's students or those doing research papers on professional doctorates or taught elements in PhD programmes.

Second, as part of their new regulatory regimes many universities are now insisting that supervisors of doctoral students should normally have a doctorate themselves. We think that, whilst desirable, this is significantly less important than that the supervisor is an established researcher who has a good understanding of the doctoral research process.

Finally, another increasingly common and sensible requirement is that academics should first undertake supervisory work alongside an experienced colleague. Generally, it's a bad idea to be a principal and especially a sole supervisor if you haven't seen the whole process through to completion of a thesis at least once, playing a real part in the work done.

How do I actually get started on doctoral supervision?

Students end up being matched with supervisors through a number of routes, some better than others.

- You may have taught or supervised a really good undergraduate or master's student. They want to go on to do research work broadly in your area and you both feel that you can work together.

> Ken is an experienced teacher and established researcher with his own PhD. He supervised Bill, an MBA student, for his dissertation which was awarded a distinction – the highest possible grade. Bill subsequently applied for and obtained a university scholarship to do a one-year research training master's, in which the dissertation is a pilot study followed by a PhD. Ken and Bill knew that they worked well together and Ken was the only suitable supervisor in the intended area of the research. However, Ken had not yet supervised any doctoral students. The director of postgraduate research degrees decided that Ken should be Bill's MA dissertation supervisor and arranged for Ken to go on the university's supervisors' training course at the same time. The supervisory team for the PhD consisted of Ken's head of department (an experienced supervisor) as the principal supervisor and Ken himself as second supervisor.

- Students who are completing the taught element of a PhD or professional doctorate may approach you and ask you to supervise/advise them.
- Your department or faculty may have systems for routing enquiries from prospective PhD students through to the most appropriate supervisor(s) for you to comment on their suitability for doctoral work and their interest for you.
- A prospective student, who has found you because they are interested in your work, may approach you directly. Such people may be colleagues, people who have read your work or people who have heard you speak at conferences and suchlike. As a matter of courtesy to the colleagues who run your doctoral programme, and because it is good practice, you must get serious applicants to engage with the formal processes even if you know that such applicants will eventually end up as your students.
- In poor doctoral programmes, students are accepted without much idea on anybody's part as to who will supervise them. These unfortunate students are then 'allocated' a supervisor or supervisory team. Often,

for both the students and the supervisors, these arranged if not forced marriages prove to be deeply unsatisfactory. We come back below to the whole issue of the formation of student–supervisor relationships.

- A senior colleague in your area may approach you and suggest that you share the supervision of a particularly suitable new student with them. This can be a really supportive and helpful way of getting you started on supervision.

Seteney is a junior lecturer in sociology, who completed her PhD with Zhang a few years ago. She and Zhang now work in the same university, where Zhang is a professor, albeit in a different department. Some time ago a prospective new student, Philippe, approached Zhang, having read her work while he was an undergraduate. He was successful in gaining a scholarship to undertake his PhD and has now begun his research training. Zhang suggested to Seteney that, since her interests were close to Philippe's, she should join the supervisory team. Zhang is Phillipe's principal supervisor and Seteney is the second supervisor. Zhang and Seteney do every supervision session together.

Given what we have said about the importance and the closeness of the student–supervisor relationship, it is crucial that at this stage both you and the student are confident that you like each other, can work together and that you have complementary skills and needs. You have to ask yourself, 'Is this a partnership that's going to work?' After all, it may last a lot longer than many marriages and other significant intimate relationships.

As the more experienced partner in this relationship, you are chiefly responsible for ensuring that it at least has the potential to work. So how do you do this? There are a number of different things that you may need to do if you don't already know each other through a previous pedagogic relationship.

Your first step must be to have a conversation with your prospective student. Ideally, this will be face to face, but if that is impossible, by telephone or email. This first conversation needs to be about what the student's abilities and interests are, what their expertise is and how their interests match yours.

At this stage, if you feel that the student is not ready for doctoral work, you need to give them appropriate advice. It might be to undertake further taught study, to read themselves into their proposed field more or to give up the idea of a doctorate completely. If you judge that they are ready to undertake this kind of endeavour, but that your interests do not match theirs, or that for some other reason you are not able to work with them, then it is better to refer them elsewhere. In such a situation the ethical thing to do is to direct them towards someone who is more suited to their particular topic either at your own university or another one.

If you are a relatively junior member of staff, do not feel intimidated or be cajoled into accepting students who are unsuitable. Sadly, you may come under pressure to accept such students from those anxious to meet student admission targets and suchlike. You should remember that whatever pressures you come under, as supervisor you are the person who will have ultimate responsibility for that student's progress and welfare.

In similar vein, do not take students on against your better judgement because you feel sorry for them. In the medium and long term you do no-one any favours by accepting them on to a programme of study that they cannot succeed on.

In thinking about whether a prospective student's interests match your own, you need to think about how far away from your own direct research interests you can, and should, supervise. You should keep in mind you that you will never (or extremely rarely) find a perfect match with your own interests. It's best to look for complementary interests – you do not need clones as research students. You need to feel enthusiastic about the student's proposed research, but it does not necessarily have to be research that would be your own first choice.

How far away from your own interests you decide to supervise will depend in part on the nature of your own work and thinking. If you tend to be fairly eclectic, broad-ranging and interdisciplinary in your own research, then you can probably supervise further away from your direct interests than if you are someone who prefers to work within a tight disciplinary framework and range of topics.

As you gain confidence as a supervisor, you may feel able to work with research students further away from your own direct interests or, indeed, it may be something that's forced on you by unfortunate circumstances.

Nathan was a part-time PhD student in the area of organisational studies. Towards the end of his period of registration, at the point at which he should have been drawing his thesis together, his supervisor went on long-term sick leave. After an interregnum, in which no suitable supervisor in the area of organisational studies could be found, the director of research degrees for the faculty agreed to become his supervisor. She was a professor of marketing and had no experience of supervising in Nick's area. However, Nick had good data, was familiar with the literature and was an excellent student. Where he needed help was in organising his material, conducting his analysis and writing the thesis. His new supervisor sought advice as needed from a more senior colleague with experience in Nick's field. He has now completed his PhD, passing with flying colours.

It may be that you think that the student's proposed research is not viable but that, with suitable adjustment, it could make a good project. Don't be afraid to engage with the prospective student to make these necessary adjustments. Be cautious, however, about the extent to which you urge them to change their topic. After all, it is their project and they have to want to do it.

It may be that the prospective student will require supervisory input additional to that which you can provide. At this point you should consider how it could be made available. It might be that a colleague, in your own department, another faculty or even another university, could be recruited as an additional supervisor.

Pamela wanted to build on her successful MA dissertation for her doctoral research. She was very keen to be supervised by Ruth, who had taught her on the MA. Although both Pamela and Ruth were interested in the broad issues, Pamela's particular topic was significantly outside Ruth's area of expertise. Ruth felt that she did not know enough of the literature to be able to supervise Pamela on her own. The more junior member of staff who had supervised Pamela's MA dissertation and who did have the specific expertise needed, but no experience of PhD supervision, joined the team as Pamela's second supervisor.

In these initial conversations with prospective students you must stress to them that doing a doctorate is a long-term commitment that involves hard work, is potentially isolating and can have a significant impact on people's family lives. Unfortunately, some prospective students (and part-time ones in particular) have little cognisance of what a PhD actually involves. You are doing them a disservice by not stressing to them how hard it is going to be. If, for example, they have an onerous work load, a demanding professional job, poor health or heavy family responsibilities, then doing a PhD may be beyond what they can manage physically, emotionally or in terms of time commitment. This is something that you cannot decide for people – sometimes, if they are very determined, they will do a PhD against all the odds.

On a similar note, sometimes people think they want to do a PhD but it is not really the right course of action for them. For example, we have had approaches from people who were already experienced researchers, who had supervised doctoral research, but who, for some reason, felt that they wanted to get a doctorate themselves. It may be possible for such people to undertake a doctorate by publication, which normally involves writing a commentary explaining how an appropriate selection of your academic publications hangs together. One group of people who may feel they want to embark on a PhD but who really shouldn't are those who have a particular political, moral or religious axe to grind or a personal agenda not amenable to academic research. Such people would be better advised to write articles or a book making their case.

Finally, some prospective students will need additional support of one kind or another if they are to get through the process. Some research projects undertaken by students may necessitate expensive equipment or other resources. Some may have some sort of impairment or mental health problem and need additional help with access of all kinds or facilitation of their study. Some students may need to acquire particular skills such as learning a foreign language. Before you take any such students on, make absolutely sure that you and your institution can help them to meet the requirements of their project and their particular needs.

In the following chapter we aim to set out some of the basic skills and information that we think you might need to help you to start supervisory work, or to improve your current practice.

6 Postgraduate Research Supervision (II) Getting and Keeping them Going

In this chapter we take you through the various stages of supervision. We are using the supervision of PhDs as a case study, because any kind of postgraduate research project involves similar stages – although how complex each stage is will clearly differ according to the level and demands of the degree it forms part of. The chapter ends with a brief consideration of some of the wider aspects of the supervisory role.

Getting students going

You have accepted your first student(s), they have a project, and now they are about to come to see you for their first ever supervision – how do you get them going on the long process of doing a PhD? At this stage in the process the student will probably feel as if they are at the base camp of Mount Everest with no ropes or other equipment and certainly no map. Your job as supervisor is to help them break the task down into manageable bites and to order the work so they don't go crazy.

Common problems

Some common problems that we have encountered with new PhD students are:

- They are filled with enthusiasm and want nothing more than to start immediately on their data collection. For obvious reasons, this is a really bad idea. You need to restrain them (sometimes with difficulty) whilst maintaining their enthusiasm as you get them to do the necessary preliminary literature-based and theoretical work.

- Often the same sort of student really resists becoming engaged in theoretical debates, which they find hard and/or classify as 'irrelevant'.
- They have only a partial or naive understanding of the knowledge fields in which their proposed research is situated. Consequently they may over-estimate what it would be possible for them to achieve. These students may be those who, at the other end of the process, find difficulty finishing because they seek all-knowing perfection in their work. Conversely, they may underestimate what is achievable and set themselves too low a target.
- There are some students who believe that their doctoral research will change the world in some significant way. This is another kind of over-estimation of what can be done with a PhD and demonstrates that they do not understand the purposes of it. Such students should be encouraged to reconfigure their ambitions more realistically early on if they are to avoid severe disappointment and cynicism later.
- In a similar way, students rarely understand the standard of work required at this level. After all, they are likely to have little or no direct experience on which to base their judgements. Most commonly, they lack confidence about their abilities and the level at which they are working. This is easier to deal with than those students who underestimate the standard required.
- Almost invariably the research topics of new students are too huge and their questions are insufficiently focused. An early task in supervision is to give students the confidence to feel that they can narrow their topic and focus their questions and that it will still constitute a valid PhD.

Students at this stage may find reading *Getting Started on Research* particularly useful.

Handy hints for things to do in the early stages of research supervision

There are some things that we have found useful, either for the first supervision or soon after:

1. Each and every supervisory relationship is different. There are no set rules on how to conduct these and you and the student have to work out what works for you all. Both supervisors and students have legitimate needs and expectations here.

At the first supervision meeting, discuss how you will conduct the supervision process and agree on matters such as roughly how often you will meet and what you expect of them and they can expect of you. If you are co-supervising with someone else, this is the point at which you need to discuss with the student and the other supervisor(s) what the roles of each person will be.

2. We strongly recommend that you get your students writing from the very start. We make it clear in the first supervision that we will not normally see our students unless they have sent us some written work, no matter how brief. You will need to agree with the student how long before your meetings you need to receive their written work. Obviously the nature and content of this work will vary and the length is likely to increase as time goes on.

3. It is very important for you and your student to keep good records of all your meetings. This acts as a protection for both of you and, more importantly, an *aide memoire* for your subsequent meetings and work. We favour systems where the student is the person who compiles the formal record of the meeting and gives all their supervisors a copy. This encourages good practice on their part and also saves busy academics the work. Furthermore, making the student prepare the record enables you, as supervisor, to verify that your understandings are shared. You might want to keep your own notes, for your own purposes, on the supervision and on how the student is progressing.

Many places have formal ways of keeping records, which require the student and/or supervisor to fill in a form. The student has to complete this and send copies to their supervisor(s) and the Research Degrees Office. Debbie has disciplined her students into sending her (and other supervisors) an email memo after each supervision summarising what was discussed and agreed at the meeting. Similarly, at the end of each supervision session Jane and her students agree on what they have agreed on and then the student emails this agreement to Jane. She also asks her students to prepare agendas for each supervision meeting.

Before the end of each supervision you need to agree on the date, time and place of your next meeting and you need to make sure that it is in your diary. The formal record should of course also note this. At the later stages, when students are writing intensively, your arrangements may be much more contingent. In any case, you and the student must record the arrangements made.

Whatever methods you adopt, the early supervisory meetings are the places to establish these good practices. It is important that these formal and informal record-keeping processes become second nature.

4. Your student's research proposal should include an initial timetable for the work to be undertaken. At this stage, you will need to put more detail into this and regularly revisit it so that you and the student together can monitor progress. Remember that it's a bad plan that can't be modified. With something as complex and amorphous as a PhD, it is very unusual to be able to schedule tasks for long periods ahead with any degree of exactitude.

5. You should strongly encourage your students to keep a research journal – or even insist that they do so. We have written, at length, in *Getting Started on Research*, about the uses of such a journal. We would recommend that you look at that book to see what kinds of uses it can be put to. We would suggest that you ask students to bring their research journals to supervisions both for their own note-taking during the meeting, and so that they have to hand a record of what they have been doing and thinking. Otherwise, like the small child asked what they did at school today, they might unhelpfully reply 'Nothing,' or 'Reading.'

6. At an early stage you should help your students to develop good habits of, and systems for, note-taking, filing, keeping records and self-organisation. We discuss all this in detail in *Getting Started on Research*.

7. Increasingly, universities are insisting that doctoral students undertake some form of formal research training at an early stage in their doctoral studies. This follows well established practice in US universities. Early research supervision meetings are an excellent place to discuss students' individual research training needs and to identify how these will be met.

8. Students should be strongly encouraged to participate in the wider research culture of their institutions. By this we mean that they should look out for and attend research seminars, not only in their direct area of study but also in cognate or related areas and even in areas unrelated to what they themselves are doing. It's good for students to have broad interests beyond their own particular research and they may pick up surprising and helpful information, knowledge or insights at such seminars, which are also good places for networking. This can sometimes be really hard for part-time

students, those doing PhDs at a distance or those with, for example, childcare responsibilities. As a supervisor it's important to lobby for appropriate arrangements for people in such circumstances.

9. At an appropriate point, it can be a good idea to suggest to students that they look at some completed PhD theses. You will need to give them some guidance as to what they're looking for. You also need to exercise caution: an unconfident student could feel completely undermined if asked to look at a completed PhD thesis too early. By the same token, an over-confident student might find such an experience beneficially salutary.

You may have an excellent group of doctoral students. However, they are not foolproof. Further, no matter how good their students are, supervisors remain responsible for making sure that they are making the right sort of progress.

As a supervisor there are three sorts of structures and constraints on your students that you need to be aware of:

- Research education (formal and informal).
- The need for the sort of informal structuring/guidance that you and your fellow supervisors have to provide (especially in the early phases).
- Formal monitoring and/or progression exams and requirements.

We discuss each of these below.

What is research education?

Different countries and universities provide different levels of generic formal research education or training for PhD students. In some institutions, some or all of it is mandatory. As a supervisor you must familiarise yourself with what is available and with any formal requirements that your students are subject to. An important part of your role is to advise your students on what constitutes the best research training for their particular needs.

We have encountered supervisors who thoroughly resent their students having to do such training. It's almost as if they see it as an insult to their professional prowess. These are often not the best supervisors. If you do have objections to or criticisms of the research education offered to your students, make sure that they are well founded and that you actually do something about them. We feel that research education is, in principle, beneficial for all students, provided it is well conceived and delivered.

We like those courses best where the work and assignments are contextualised within the students' intended research topics. This helps to overcome a feeling common to many students that research courses are nothing more than frustrating hurdles designed solely to prevent them from 'getting on with their work'. Formal courses can also give students at the start of their research a certain degree of structure – especially if the work they do on them is made meaningful within the context of their own intended or actual research.

Unfortunately, it is also our experience that some research training courses are *unbelievably* bad. For example, some treat the students like undergraduates and fail to teach at a doctoral level. When forced to take such courses, students are right to see them as an obstacle rather than as a way of acquiring necessary knowledge and skills. If you and your doctoral students don't like what is on offer, you and your colleagues might consider mounting some courses yourselves if it is possible.

Part-time students need extra consideration here. The scheduling of formal (and possibly compulsory) research training courses can place real obstacles in their way to obtaining a PhD.

At Jenny's university the needs of part-time and distance research students are taken seriously. For example, the entire structured programme for doctoral students is offered in two slots, one for full-time students and one for part-time students. For distance students regular tele-conferences are conducted so that they can talk to each other in ways similar to those who are doing face-to-face on-campus sessions. The university has developed a statement of minimum resources to which all students are entitled and in so doing it has ensured that distance students have the same order of entitlement as face-to-face students. There are lessons to be learnt here for less accommodating institutions, which would do well to take heed of such good practice.

Different sorts of disciplines will have different potential research education needs. You might helpfully distinguish between generic skills and subject-specific knowledge and skills. Formal research courses can be invaluable for a number of reasons above and beyond those noted earlier.

- In areas that typically recruit students who may not necessarily have social science/arts/humanities backgrounds (such as business and management, health and social care, education), there may be a real need to give students a good grounding in epistemological issues. A common fault in such fields is that research is descriptive and un- or under-theorised. Courses can help avert this.
- Some forms of research may necessitate students updating or acquiring particular skills.
- Where students are 'discipline-hopping' they may need substantive education in new fields.
- Generic training in methods of data collection and analysis may open students' minds to research methods that they had not conceived of or had little previous knowledge about.
- Some students, especially those returning to study, may need to develop their IT skills. In particular, research students may well need training in bibliographic databases, Web skills, library skills and other data analysis software aids. Librarians often offer wonderful courses to help students (and others) to meet such needs.
- Research courses can help to overcome the social and work isolation and the sense of inadequacy that many PhD students feel by putting them into contact with others in a similar position. Cross-disciplinary courses can have the added advantage of helping students to meet others from outside their immediate fields, thereby widening their intellectual horizons.
- Students may benefit from taking courses on such matters as intellectual property, commercialisation, career building, university-level teaching and so on.

It is a good practice to discuss your students' research education needs at regular intervals with them. Make sure that you are well informed about what the institution can offer and where else they can get the education that they need. But encourage your students to take responsibility for defining what they need help with and sourcing the requisite courses. It is unreasonable for students to expect you to be the expert in all such areas and their only source of assistance and training. Students may need financial help if the requisite courses are externally held. We think that good departments, within reason, should pay such fees or they should make it clear to the students at the outset that it will not be possible.

> Ruth was doing a PhD in Latin American studies at a wealthy university in the USA. She spoke some Spanish, but it wasn't sufficient for her to undertake her research. Her institution paid for her to go to Mexico to spend five weeks undertaking an intensive Spanish course at the end of the first year of her taught doctoral studies.
>
> Maggie is doing her PhD on the experiences of Deaf people at work. She needed to learn British Sign Language, the main language of the British Deaf community. Her institution paid for her to attend the relevant courses at a neighbouring university.

As well as formal courses, remember that there are plenty of sources for more informal education. Seminars and conferences offer good opportunities for students to learn about research. It is helpful for a student if their supervisor knows which conferences are particularly useful and student-friendly. While the large conventions may be good for networking, they are rarely the best places for students to learn from others or to present their own work.

Students might also wish to establish their own small reading/support groups as a form of mutual education and training. If/when you have a big enough cohort of doctoral students, they may find it helpful if you organise regular informal meetings at which they can raise issues of concern or interest to them for mutual consideration and build up a sense of solidarity.

Don't underestimate the informal training and education that supervisors give their students. For instance, the best way of helping people to learn how to write is undoubtedly to sit with them and demonstrate the processes of planning, structuring and composition.

Helping students to structure and develop their work in the early stages

A key aspect of supervision, especially in the early stages, is to help students develop their ideas; sequencing their work in useful ways. This is not a linear process, but rather an iterative one with plenty of overlap between different kinds of work. However, for the sake of clarity, we will deal with the different things that students need to do in the first few months of their research for their doctorate as if the stages were discrete. This is dealt with at much greater length in *Getting Started on Research*. If you want more detail than we give in this section, we would recommend that you read that book in addition to this one.

Students need to:

- *Gain a good idea of what they're going to do.* At the earliest stages they need to identify the field within which their particular topic falls and begin to understand the nature of the intellectual space within which they are operating. For this reason, they will need to read widely in that field to start with. They need to have a rough map in their minds of where their topics and questions are situated. This is best developed by wide reading. It is your job to direct them towards suitable initial reading but it is their job to follow it up and extend your initial list.
- *Read within their chosen field*, with a focus on their own particular topics and questions. Once they have a mind map of their field they are ready to read in a more focused way. At this point they need to know what is already available in the public story about their topic that can help them answer the research questions they have set themselves.
- *Read their way into the most immediately pertinent literature.* They need to develop a real sense of what the wider debates in their chosen field are. This will involve looking at key authors and thinkers, methodological issues and generally getting to know the 'intellectual space' to which they wish to belong. However, it's a poor farmer who allows her cattle to graze all over the field at will: students have to be encouraged to graze with a purpose and in carefully defined patches. Such critical grazing is essential for the development of a critical gaze. That said, we also believe that a certain amount of 'getting lost' in the literature is the sort of activity

that both encourages people to think their way through things in a flexible way and also, quite often, leads to serendipitous thoughts, finds and insights.

Common problems are both grazing too widely and narrowing too quickly. There are also real problems with 'recency effects' – where the most influential thinker in the student's life is that last one that they read.

- *Regularly revisit their research proposal.* As students become *au fait* with the literature and debates relevant to their topics, they need to revisit their research proposal and iteratively refine it to ensure that it remains relevant and useful to what they are doing. In particular, they need to consider whether their research questions need adjustment – which may be minor tweaking or represent a more major refocusing of the research.

In addition, as the work progresses, students need to plan well ahead how they will identify, access and collect the material that they need and how it will be analysed.

As part of guiding students through the research process, we get all of our students to regularly revisit and revise their research proposals, paying particular attention to their research questions.

- *Be taught how to read actively and take notes from their reading.* In *Writing for Publication* we talk about the need for researchers to read widely and to engage actively with the texts they are reading. This is, of course, just as essential for research students, and one of the most useful things you can help them with in the early phases of their research is how to do it. Taking systematic notes is an essential part of active reading, and your students must devise or learn their own systems for doing so. Carrie Paechter uses one such system and always shows her research students how it works very early on in their degree. We include it here as an example that you and your students might think about.

Carrie's note-taking system came to her from Arthur Lucas, who was the professor in her department in her first job, in the days before bibliographic databases were easily available and in common use. As it was such a good system, she has adapted it for use with electronic bibliographic databases and teaches it to her research students.

▶

▶ The system has three parts. The first part is in a series of hardback notebooks, all of them the same size and colour (in her case, black) and lined. As she finishes each notebook she numbers it with a sticker on the spine. In her current book, she makes notes from whatever she is reading. Each item starts on a new page, and if she is reading more than one thing at a time she leaves a sufficient number of pages to make the notes that she thinks she will need, so that the different texts don't get muddled up. At the beginning of the notes about a particular piece she gives it a unique number. So the first piece in book No. 14 is called 14/1.

She also writes down the bibliographic details, including author, date of publication, source (e.g. book or journal), title of the piece, place of publication and publisher, ISBN or ISSN, page numbers for chapter or articles, and the library class mark if appropriate. For Web pages she notes the date accessed and the URL as well. This gives her all the information that she may need if she refers to the text in something she later writes and publishes. It also lets her find the item again easily.

Her notes are relatively brief, though they may include the occasional direct quote, clearly indicated, together with the page number(s) from which she copied it. For the most part, however, she notes only the key ideas and main lines of argument.

The second part of her system is a bibliographic database kept using a special piece of software on her computer (see below). On this database, once she has finished reading the text, she enters:

- All the bibliographic details noted above.
- Keywords that she has extracted from the text.
- Sometimes, but not always, a few notes or her own abstract of the paper.
- A note of where she found the text, for example, whether she owns it, which library she borrowed it from (including the library class mark), whether she has a copy of a journal article and so on.
- A note of the number of the notebook in which she made the original notes.

The final part of her system is the filing of her books and article offprints. The former she shelves in alphabetical order, by first author, the latter in a filing cabinet, also by first author. ▶

> This system enables her to do a number of things:

- She can go to her database and quickly find relevant works by typing in appropriate key words.
- From the information in her database she can find her full notes in her notebooks quickly and easily and remind herself of the article or book she is interested in.
- She knows pretty much what she was doing at the time when she was reading things because they appear in chronological order in her notebooks. This means that, as her ideas have changed over the years, she can look at her previous notes and remember what was uppermost in her mind at the time.
- She knows where to find the text if she wants to go back to the original.

Helping students meet formal requirements

We have already discussed the ways in which universities are increasingly seeking to structure a student's doctoral work by putting in place formal milestones and monitoring processes. We have also explained why we welcome these moves with modified rapture.

Your role as a supervisor in these processes and requirements is crucial and, for the sake of your students or your own career, you cannot afford to screw up here. You have to take these things seriously and ensure that you and your students:

- Do what is required, when it is required.
- Do what is required to at least the expected minimum standard.
- Do not wait to be chased or cajoled into compliance. This puts out your colleagues who are responsible for such processes, and can also reflect badly on your students.
- Take seriously the presentational aspects of these requirements. For instance, if the requirement is to submit work in progress, make sure that the presentation is professional and not an insult or an inconvenience to those examining it.
- Take care in using your discretion (if you have any) in matters such as the selection of examiners for interim oral exams. An undeserved

rough ride for a student at this stage can seriously damage their confidence. Equally, a good examiner can really help you and the student to develop the work.

- Take these processes seriously. If a student is not progressing well then you are not necessarily doing him/her any favours in 'easing them through' formal hurdles so that they may have an even bigger fall later on.

Gargi was an overseas doctoral student whose parents were very anxious for her to obtain a PhD. She struggled constantly with the work and made poor progress for no obvious reason other than that her heart was not in it and she was therefore not capable of giving it the attention it needed.

Her supervisor was not only research-inactive but also had little idea about university progression requirements and why they were in place. He arranged for Gargi's progression examination to be conducted by a nice chap and friendly colleague. The examiner expressed serious reservations about Gargi's progress in his report. However, instead of recommending that she withdraw from the programme or do an MPhil he allowed her to progress and recommended that she should be given an extra year because of her slow progress.

Gargi continued to fail at her research. Eventually, after four years during which she had paid high fees for full-time study, the professor in charge of the doctoral programme decided to terminate her registration. Gargi was offered the possibility of being registered for an MPhil and being given exemption from the minimum registration period if she worked informally with a new supervisor and completed a near final draft of her dissertation. She is currently working, as an unregistered student, towards an MPhil.

If Gargi's original supervisor had done his job properly and the progression examiner had not acted out of misplaced kindness, Gargi's situation would not have become so dire, expensive and distressing for her. She was unnecessarily placed in a position where she was distressed and humiliated by being removed from the programme.

How do I help students to keep on keeping on?

Maintaining momentum in research can be a problem for PhD students. Doing a PhD is a long-term, often lonely and essentially difficult task. Students may understandably cling to comfort zones in such circumstances. A common one is to carry on collecting data well past the optimal point for stopping.

Students may also endlessly invent tasks that, in their view, are absolutely essential to do but which have the real and probably unconscious purpose of delaying actually getting on with what they need to do. Everyone does this to some extent, including us. The job of the supervisor is to help students contain this kind of activity at reasonable levels. Deciding that you can't start writing until you have been out to the stationery shop and bought a new coloured gel pen is one thing, but deciding that you have to undertake a new six-month-long archival search is quite another.

Real problems can arise as students start to bury themselves in a field and accumulate large quantities of material. Often the process of analysing and making sense of it all can appear overwhelming. Students in this situation may avoid what they see as an insurmountable task by insisting that they need to carry on collecting more material, thereby making their dilemma worse.

Developing your theoretical thinking is a really challenging and difficult process for everyone. Students are usually initially perplexed at how to bring their theoretical insights from their reading together with the material they have. It's helpful, at this point, to encourage students to locate and read examples of where this is done well in order to see how they themselves might do it. This is one of the biggest challenges of the whole research process.

One common tendency is for students to be unsure that they themselves have got anything worthwhile to say. Such students often produce writing that consists of the confident recitation of synthesised literature, tentatively illustrated by little snippets of their own work. The trick for the supervisor is to help the student see the value of the work that they have done and help them develop a confident voice.

Another common motivational problem is that students may have a real reluctance to write and to write often. Such students often feel that they cannot start writing until they know everything, have collected every conceivable piece of material and have every idea perfectly conceptualised. Only when all their ducks are in a row will they start shooting. Supervisors can play an important role here by encouraging, chivvying and, indeed, insisting that students develop good writing practices at an early stage. We talk more about helping students develop their writing below and about the writing process at length in *Writing for Publication*.

Finally, it is worth saying that students often go through periods of feeling resentful and angry with their supervisors. They may even hate you or hide when they see you coming down the corridor. As with any long-term and intense relationship, this is perfectly normal and you should not be cast down when or if it happens. The gamut of the dynamics of the supervisor–student relationship will vary from nurturing and consoling to cajoling, chivvying and getting really tough and demanding. It's normal.

Handy hints for helping students start writing and to write well

As we have just said, students may have a real reluctance to write and to write often. Their second big problem can be the need to have done everything and thought of everything before they start writing. These students often refer to 'writing up' their thesis. They fail to see writing for what it is – an on-going integral part of the research process.

1. Writing is often something that students feel anxious about. Dealing with this can be difficult for those supervisors who, themselves, find writing problematic or worrisome. Helping students to write can actually help supervisors to improve their own writing skills and practices. This is because the process of articulating how to do it and the sharing of writing experience informs your own thinking. Thinking about students' work makes you read your own more critically.

2. Having other people read their work can make students feel very exposed and vulnerable. For this reason you should never ever, under any circumstances, set out to make a student feel stupid about their writing. They are likely to feel bad enough about their writing without you making it worse.

Shamila is the best writer that Davina has ever met. When she became Davina's student, first during her MA and then as a doctoral student, Shamila already wrote with a fluency and elegance that Davina could only long for. She is also a remarkably original thinker and nuanced theorist. Even her rough field notes were of publishable standard. When she handed her work in, Davina's feedback took the form of further ideas to develop, but virtually never about style, composition or structure of the writing. Shamila noticed that Davina's other students had their work returned to them with far more extensive comments on such matters. She decided, erroneously, that this was because Davina hated her writing.

Esther is also a talented writer. However, she had the misfortune of being allocated a supervisor whose behaviour at every supervision session sapped her interest in her topic and her confidence in herself as a writer and a thinker. During the entire process he never once offered her any positive feedback on her work. Over the period of her supervision, as her confidence in her own abilities diminished, so did the quality of her writing. Her supervisor's criticisms thus became even more shrill, further diminishing her capacity to produce high-quality work, to the extent where she became almost paralysed. She was fortunate to have access to other sources of support which enabled her to complete her degree and get a good mark, though not as good as her potential suggested it would be.

Refrain from rude comments and, above all, avoid a red pen for them. Using one will make your students feel like they are ten years old, getting their unsuccessful maths homework back. Better to invest in some nice coloured gel pens (purple, green, whatever) and keep the red for your own writing.

Ian was in the final stages of drafting his thesis. He had recently had to change supervisors because of circumstances outside his control. ▶

> ▶ His new supervisor devoted a lot of effort to helping Ian to structure and write his thesis. He was appreciative of the fact that Ian was quick to learn the skills needed for this purpose and Ian was delighted to have found someone who could help him in his writing. One day he confided to his supervisor that he had shown his wife one of the returned draft chapters, pointing out that his supervisor had unthinkingly, hurriedly and untypically written 'inept' in the margin against a particular piece of text. Far from showing the sympathy he expected, his wife merely replied, 'Well, if he ever writes anything complimentary you'll know he means it.'

3. There are remarkably few people whose writing appears effortlessly beautiful. You will be lucky if you get to supervise one of them in a whole career. Writing, like bricklaying or plastering, is an apparently prosaic skill that can actually be developed only by frequent and regular practice.

   Try to build good writing practices into your supervisory activities. Encouraging students to keep good research journals can be an excellent way of getting them into the regular writing habit.

4. Students may feel defensive about their writing to the point where they can't listen to constructive criticism. Or they may not want to show you any writing until they think it is nearly perfect. To these students, you need to say:

Write it, then get it right. Don't get it right, get it written.

The more writing your students do, and the more constructive criticism you and others give them on their writing, the better they will become at it. They need to learn, if they don't already understand, that writing is an iterative process. You should encourage them to show their work to their fellow students, their partners, their friends, other members of staff and any other friendly critical readers they can find, as well as to yourself.

5. Not only does frequent writing improve students' skill, it's also an important way in which they can achieve real unity with their materials, sort out their ideas, articulate their thoughts, decide where they've gone wrong, discover the holes in their theory, work out what they really think and so on.

   The process of writing is essential to the development of productive dialogue between the supervisor and the student and between research materials and theory. Without those dialogues, it is not possible to write a good final thesis. It is only when you read your students' work that you really begin to understand what they are thinking. Conversations, important though they are, are simply too slippery and imprecise as a tool for developing a thesis.

6. One of your responsibilities as a supervisor is to help your students develop their own particular writing or authorial voice. They need to be fully present in their writing. Eventually, anything they write will be recognisably theirs. In many areas of the arts, humanities and social sciences these days, it is conventional for authors to use the first person. We think that this is a very good development, since it encourages honesty in writing and makes it harder to adopt a quasi-godlike, pseudo-objective stance. However, many students suffer from 'physics envy' and will thus find it uncomfortable at first, particularly if they have had it drummed into them at school and/or university that they should distance themselves by writing in the third person.

7. The PhD thesis is a very particular and peculiar genre – and almost unique in being written for an audience of only a very few people (consisting of the supervisor(s) and examiners). Students obviously need to learn how to write according to PhD generic rules but they also have to be able to write for other audiences.

   Whilst doing their doctoral research, students should also learn to write for publication and begin to publish. This is essential for their future career prospects. The best theses are designed such that papers can be relatively easily generated in parallel to the writing of the thesis at each stage. It can immeasurably increase students' confidence in their own work to have had it accepted for publication, whole or in part, prior to the completion of the thesis. Indeed, it is often the case that one of the key criteria for passing a PhD is that it is 'publishable whole or in part'. The student who has already published doctoral work in reputable places prior to being examined has, by definition, met this criterion.

> Jane was a well organised and hard-working PhD student who completed her thesis ahead of time. Her supervisor put her in touch with a reputable academic publisher, who commissioned her thesis as a book. Jane was able to use the time that good progress on the thesis had saved in order write her book. By the time she was examined, the book was already in press. Thus Jane was able to go into her oral examination knowing that she had already satisfied a key criterion of a successful PhD – that the thesis was publishable whole or in part.

A word of caution is necessary here. There are some universities where the regulations prevent students from publishing from their theses in advance of examination. Obviously such regulations must not be ignored. Our advice to students is to avoid those universities or lobby for a change in the rules. We would urge supervisors to put the case to their university that it is cutting off their nose to spite their face and out of line with most current practice. Not having published puts students at a significant competitive disadvantage in the job market compared with those who have.

There is plenty more advice about writing styles, practices and publishing in *Writing for Publication*.

Finishing and beyond

The finishing phase in the doctoral process necessitates helping the student to mould all their research and writing into the completed thesis. The thesis must hang together as a coherent and convincing story. In short, the thesis must have a thesis – that is, an argument. In Figure 1 we illustrate the metaphor used by one of Rebecca's colleagues, Charles Harvey, who compares a finished thesis to a string of pearls.

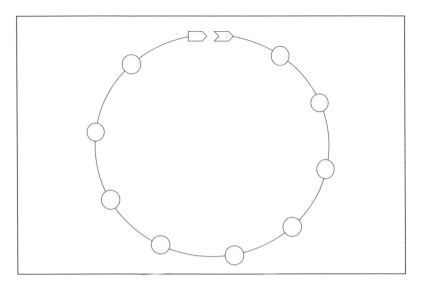

FIGURE 1   The thesis as a string of pearls. The fastenings at either end of the string are the introduction and conclusion, the chapters are the pearls and the string is the line of argument that runs through all of them. Of course, the clasps have to match perfectly to make the string whole. Reading the thesis should be analagous to a journey round this string of pearls. The reader starts at the introduction, in which the purpose of the thesis and the nature of the journey are set out clearly. The argument then progresses through a series of discrete but connected chapters, eventually arriving at the conclusion, which returns to the introduction and ties the whole together. Like a string of pearls, the thesis should be a thing of beauty.

Students who are within spitting distance of finishing should develop a detailed and realistic timetable for the final completion of their thesis. They should start this by working backwards from their intended submission date and should factor in time for slippage.

Students frequently underestimate the amount of time that the technical aspects and tidying involved in the final production of the thesis will take. Matters such as checking the bibliography, pagination, labelling of diagrams, images or figures, compiling tables of contents, checking any appendices and so on can take days, even weeks of tedious work. It is made more difficult because the student is usually exhausted by the intellectual effort expended up to this point. In addition, many students, by this stage, may have started a new and demanding job, and simply finding the hours to do the work can be difficult. Encourage your students to factor this finishing phase into their scheduling of their work.

Completing a thesis is very hard work and the final stages are particularly demanding. Students are nearly always totally exhausted, physically, mentally and emotionally, by that point. An added dimension of the finishing phase is dealing with the associated difficult emotions. These emotions may reflect a fear of finishing.

- They are about to give their thesis over for critical scrutiny and are likely to be very anxious in case it is failed or has major revisions. This is often particularly acute for the best students, who set themselves the highest standards and strive for perfection.
- It can mark the end of a very important period in their lives, which has been formative intellectually and emotionally and socially sustaining. They know who they are as a doctoral student. They may not be sure who they will be when they are no longer a student.
- They may feel apprehensive or uncertain about what the future holds. If they are going on to a new job or career they may not have the confidence to feel that they can cope and may be afraid of being 'found out' as wanting. If they are students who are continuing in another profession, they may be apprehensive about the transformative effect that their research may have had on their attitudes to their work or their lives. In similar vein, those who are returning to very different cultural environments may be concerned about how they will fit back in.

All in all, it is not surprising that many students find themselves suffering from quite serious depression as they finish their thesis and immediately afterwards. The supervisor should be there for them at this point, see them through it and encourage them to plan positively for the short and medium term. Good advice to students is to get them to go on vacation immediately after they have handed their thesis in, if this is humanly possible. At the very least, even if they can afford only a long weekend away, it will do them good.

Planning for finishing may also have to include preparing for an oral examination and should always include thinking about future publications arising from the work and future research plans, if any. Planning publications and thinking about research possibilities arising from the thesis are, in fact, good preparation for any oral examination that the student has to go through.

Where students have to have an oral examination, they should put their thesis away for a minimum of two or three weeks before doing any preparation or planning. They need to get a bit of distance from it. Then they need to reread their thesis with a view to thinking and reminding themselves about:

- Its contribution to knowledge.
- Its originality in terms of opening up new areas of enquiry, methodology, empirical data, theory building and analysis.
- Where their work is situated within their discipline and field.
- Who would be interested in what they have done and what the likely impact of their research will be within their own intellectual field and/or among practitioner communities, policy makers or the wider public.
- With the benefit of hindsight, what they would have done differently and how.
- The 'so what?'-ness of their research.
- Future lines of enquiry suggested by their research.

These are the same sorts of questions that one has to address in writing a book proposal. They are also the kinds of question that are likely to be pursued in an oral examination. Consequently, suggesting to students that they actually should write a book proposal kills two birds with one stone: it allows them to plan for putting their thesis into wider circulation and it is good examination preparation. Another good activity for students at this point is to identify several articles that could come out of their thesis and think about where they might be published.

Once students have submitted their thesis, Jane advises her students to develop a publishing plan. This may involve a book plan, but more usually involves a series of articles. With regard to each, the following details should be developed: title; journal, proposed date of submission, abstract. Previously published articles should be included in the publishing plan because they indicate what has already been done and the direction of the subsequent publications. The benefits of the publishing plan are that it encourages students to move past the story of the whole thesis and to develop papers that can stand on their own merit. A second benefit is that distributing the publishing plan at interviews for jobs at other universities impresses selection panels.

The examination process

We'd like to add a note here for the majority of supervisors whose students' work is examined by people other than themselves. This may or may not involve an oral examination. The selection of appropriate internal and external examiners is one of the most important moments in a student's doctoral studies. It needs to be done well in advance of completion, with great care and in close consultation with the student themselves.

Make sure that the prospective examiners' own epistemological approach complements that of the student and that they are likely to understand and be sympathetic to the topic and the methods used. In addition, good examiners are people who can read a thesis from the point of view of the student's stated aims, rather than the kind of reader who thinks that everyone should do it the way they would. In general, it is our experience that examiners who are, themselves, confident and established in their research career are better at doing this than those who feel that they have something to prove. Be aware that an examiner whose work is very close to that of the student may, despite the best of intentions, find it difficult to distance themselves adequately from their own perspective, and this may disadvantage the student. Bear in mind that the higher the status of the examiner, the better the halo effect on the student when they pass. In addition, good examiners may also be willing to act as referees in future job applications, publishing projects and generally promote the student and their work.

Good examiners will read the student's work closely and be able to engage with them helpfully in discussions on publication plans and ways to take the work forward in further research. They will be simultaneously challenging and supportive. The student should have already engaged with the examiners' work in their thesis. This is one reason why you and the student should start thinking about potential examiners at least a year in advance of the intended submission date.

Obviously, if and when you become an examiner, you need to try to be like the best examiner you could wish for your own students.

Sometimes your students will be required to make major or minor revisions to their thesis before it is finally passed. If these go beyond correcting typographical errors, your involvement will be absolutely essential. You will need to help the student pick up the pieces both intellectually and emotionally and help them find practical solutions to get a prompt, positive result. Your supervision does not stop until after the thesis is passed.

Wider aspects of the supervisory role

In conclusion, we want to talk about three wider aspects of supervisory work. These are:

- Helping your students to develop a rounded professional profile.
- Being supportive and nurturing to your students.
- Maintaining good boundaries and knowing the limits of your responsibilities.

We will consider each in turn.

Helping your students to develop a rounded professional profile

Most doctoral students will either want to pursue a career as an academic or as a researcher in some other environment. For such students, you need to think about the skills and experience they will need to develop in such a way that their career prospects are optimised.

With regard to research, we have already spoken about the importance of their getting published during the PhD process. But you also need to encourage them to think about getting experience of such things as going to conferences, presenting papers, building academic networks and, indeed, finding their own place in their research community. These are all things they can get valuable experience of whilst they are your student, and you are in part responsible for facilitating it. At a practical level, you should think about doing such things for them as: co-authoring papers; attending and presenting at conferences with them; offering them research or writing opportunities; and introducing them to your circles and networks. You may also be able to help them acquire project management or administrative experience by finding them limited tasks to do on your own projects or on those of colleagues.

At a mundane level, you will be aware that universities are places where getting hold of very basic resources such as office space, a desk, filing cabinets, a computer and a car park pass can turn into a major headache. You should be aware that your full-time students, in particular, require basic resources similar to your own and you should do whatever you can to make sure that they are provided or that the student can access them.

Students who wish to pursue an academic career in teaching and research will also need to be able to demonstrate to prospective employers that they are competent teachers. All students need help in selecting and applying for appropriate teaching opportunities. They will need guidance on how to teach, and support through this particular learning curve. It shouldn't be an onerous task for the supervisor. With regard to your students, you need to keep a careful eye on the balance of their work load between teaching and research. It is all too easy, especially for inexperienced teachers, for teaching preparation and marking to expand to fill their entire working week, to the detriment of their research. In general, as a faculty member, you should be mindful of the fact that, almost invariably, students undertake such work at very low rates of pay, are frequently untrained or poorly trained and unsupported in an institutional sense. It is part of your responsibility, as a member of the university, to do what you can to minimise or end such exploitative treatment.

Being supportive and nurturing your students

You need to be aware that students are vulnerable people by nature of their relatively powerless position within universities. It is, therefore, incumbent on supervisors to be reflexive about the impact that their supervisory practices may have. Doctoral students are part of the academic community and should be treated as such. We find it helpful in our everyday dealings and personal relations with such students to think of them more as inexperienced and less senior colleagues than as 'students'.

In working with them, it is important not to try to turn them into some kind of carbon copy of yourself. They are independent people in their own right and must develop their own research and research careers. You have to get the balance right between nurturing them, and helping them to develop, and taking control of their lives and work. You are not their parent and shouldn't endlessly feel responsible for them. You can't and shouldn't want to live your life through them. You can take pleasure in their successes, but such successes should always ultimately be their own. (Good advice for parents, too.)

In good supervisory relationships your students should remain your academic friends and colleagues for the rest of your career. They should be able to rely on you for mentoring, letters of support for job applications, assistance with research funding applications and as a critical friend who continues to be willing to read their work. By the same token, as they become more confident and competent academics they will prove to be valuable critical friends to you.

Developing good boundaries and knowing the limits of your responsibilities

First and foremost, as we said in Chapter 3, you should never, ever get into your students' knickers, no matter how beguiling, gorgeous or seductive they are. Teaching generates all kinds of emotionally close and charged relationships. It is one thing to have intense and often very satisfying close pedagogical relations with your students, in which you may feel close and affectionate towards each other. It is another thing entirely to become involved with them sexually. The former is a mark of an exceptionally good teacher–student relationship. The latter represents an abuse of power by the supervisor and always has adverse consequences for the student and sometimes for both.

Second, it's important to have effective and flexible working arrangements with your research students. You might, for instance, find it nicer or more convenient to see them in your study at home. If they are part-time students, they may need to talk to you on the phone in the evening at home. At work, your research students should feel comfortable enough to drop by when they have a small thing they need to check out with you or to share something that has interested or amused them. They will most certainly need to be able to make robust and reliable arrangements with you for supervisions and other aspects of their work with you. It is appropriate for them to have your home phone number and they certainly need to be able to contact you by email. This can be especially important during any fieldwork phase, where they may encounter problems or difficulties that require urgent resolution with your help and possibly out of office hours.

Having said all that, you are not married to them (and if you are, stop supervising them NOW). They need to learn to respect your space and privacy and to know that they are not your only responsibility. In practice, if you treat them with respect, the overwhelming majority will reciprocate. You may need to agree explicitly on matters such as when it's okay to ring you at home. Don't be afraid of having such conversations – they can make for sound working relationships in the long run.

It is part of an academic's working life that, from time to time, they will have longer or shorter absences from the university. When you do, you need to make adequate and appropriate arrangements for and with your doctoral students. In some cases, this will involve nothing more than telling them that you will be away on vacation or at a conference for a limited period and checking that there are no outstanding, urgent matters looming on their horizon.

If you are going away for a longer period of study/research leave, you will need to decide whether you wish to carry on active supervision or whether it is better to arrange for a colleague to assist them in the interim. You and the student together have to make individual judgements on this. If you are in a supervisory team, it may be that the other supervisor can take full responsibility for this limited period. If you are the senior or sole supervisor and are going abroad for an extended period, you may need to make arrangements for email and/or telephone supervision. In any event, if you are going to be away for more than a couple of weeks, you need to make sure that the student is aware of a nominated and responsible individual in the department whom they can contact in an emergency or crisis.

And Finally...

We hope we have demonstrated that supervising research students is not only a complex and challenging form of teaching, but also has the potential to be very rewarding work for you as a teacher. Not only can doing such work make a substantial and positive difference to students' careers and their perspectives on their lives, but it can also have a transformative effect on your own research work. It can give you lifelong research friends, and the very process of helping others to engage with research should help you to engage more critically and reflexively with your own research practice.

Further Reading

Bates, A.W. and Poole, G. (2003) *Effective Teaching with Technology in Higher Education: Foundations for Success*, Indianapolis In: Jossey Bass Wiley. As the title suggests, this book addresses how to utilise information technology in pedagogical practice. Because the introduction of information technology into student learning is frequently driven by (usually unfounded) managerial expectations of cost cutting it may be wise to be well informed in this complex area. Rather than being a simple proselytising book, this one aims to provide a sound theoretical basis to explanations of why technology may aid teaching and learning. The book also provides practical advice on how to design and implement courses that involve the use of information technology. The text appears to be popular among those who, unlike us, are keen on such teaching modes.

Delamont, S., Atkinson, P. and Parry, O. (2004) *Supervising the Doctorate: A Guide to Success.* Maidenhead: Society for Research into Higher Education & Open University Press. This is the second edition of *Supervising the PhD* by the same authors. Its new title has been chosen to reflect the fact that they have not only updated the text, but added substantial material about professional doctorates. It is based on a combination of a major research project about doctoral supervision and the wealth of experience that Sara Delamont and Paul Atkinson have of supervising research students and running courses for them and for staff who wish to develop their supervision skills. It covers doctoral supervision across social sciences, humanities and sciences. While based on UK experience, the book is also relevant to doctoral supervison elsewhere. It contains many illustrative and exemplary vignettes drawn from experience and research and the authors offer heaps of good advice. At times, the tone can seem to be somewhat prescriptive and to assume that supervisors are able to devote themselves almost exclusively to their doctoral supervison, but the authors are careful to say that people must find their own best patterns of working together. Overall, the book is an invaluable resource for supervisors and for research students alike.

Newbie, D. and Cannon, R. (2000) *A Handbook for Teachers in Universities and Colleges*, 4th edn, London and New York: RoutledgeFalmer. This book tackles a range of issues from different types of teaching styles, class sizes, planning for a curriculum and the use of technology in the classroom to presentations in conferences and teaching in physics labs. Diverse learning styles as well as implementation models are discussed. Clear flow charts and graphics are used to illustrate how students learn. Newer areas such as 'problem-based learning' are discussed. The subject of teaching is dealt with thoroughly from aims to methodology and the respective advantages and disadvantages of each. The book is invaluable to someone who is embarking on a teaching career and discusses assessment methods as well as teaching evaluation routines. Though interesting, the book skims over each topic and would benefit from more in-depth discussion in each area, as the areas are so discrete. The work is generously peppered with cartoons and checklists driving home the key messages.

Holbrook, A. and Johnston, S. (eds) (1999) *Supervision of Postgraduate Research in Education: Review of Research in Education No. 5*, Coldstream, Vic: Australian Association for Research in Education. Although this book draws on the experiences of Australian education academics – in relation both to being supervisors and to being supervised – it actually speaks to a much wider audience than that would imply, both geographically and in disciplinary terms. Much of what these Australian writers have to say about their supervisory work and doctoral students within education applies equally to other disciplines (especially those in the social sciences). The book starts with an overview of the literature about doctoral research supervision and continues with personal and theoretical reflections on different aspects of supervision and being supervised, an extensive consideration of ethical issues in supervision, and finishes with a look to the future in relation to 'off-campus' (that is, distance) supervision and developments in postgraduate pedagogy. This book won't tell you how to do it, but is a rewarding read from which you can learn a great deal about supervising and being supervised.

Leonard, D. (2001) *A Woman's Guide to Doctoral Studies*, Buckingham: Open University Press. The book is aimed at students contemplating and engaged in a doctoral programme. Written engagingly and clearly, it tackles such practical issues such as how to select a supervisor and a university from the bewildering array of choices available in the UK, USA and Canada. It not only discusses the process of research but also the aftermath of completing a PhD and life following the examination. The problems of getting off (and staying off) the ground are scrutinised. The title is misleading because this excellent book would benefit all doctoral students, male or female, and also addresses issues such as race and nationality (home versus overseas), which may be encountered whilst studying for a degree. Anecdotal evidence is used in the form of case studies/quotations in boxes to bolster the points made about doing research, which is really helpful, and is supplemented with extra reading suggestions at the end. A really thorough book which is a pleasure to read.

Montgomery D. (ed.) (2002) *Cogs in the Classroom Factory: the Changing Identity of Academic Labour*, Westport CT: Greenwood Press. This is an academic study, rather than a guide or support book. The principal focus of this collection of essays is the subject of academic unionisation (and all that goes with it) in the context of the academic labour market in the USA. It considers matters such as casualisation, unionisation, tenure, the potentially problematic nature of professional unions (as opposed to blue-collar ones) and so on. Montgomery has a fine reputation as a labour historian and for involvement in such matters, and this book will make insightful reading for all academics, whether US-based or not.

Phillips, E.M. and Pugh, D.S. (1987) *How to get a PhD*, 3rd edn, Buckingham: Open University Press. A definitive book appealing to a wide audience, including prospective/present doctoral students, supervisors, examiners and university managers. It is the standard text for doctoral studies in the UK and is frequently referenced by other writers. It offers a wealth of practical examples, to illustrate abstract areas such as the suitability and originality of a research topic, motivation to do a PhD (including a chapter on why not to do a PhD) and so on. It also has excellent ideas to cope with preparation for the amorphous nature of the *viva*, including practical ideas such as grid techniques and mock *vivas*. The style is easy to read and includes a summary of action points at the end of each chapter.

Salmon P. (1992) *Achieving a PhD,* Stoke on Trent: Trentham Books. This book theorises the doctoral process through the stories of ten diverse doctoral students whom the author has met in different circumstances. These pen portraits are used to analyse leaning styles, objectives and procedures the students used in achieving their PhDs. The problems of these students are drawn upon to provide a model of how gender and other social relations enter the learning equation. This book draws the reader into the world of the doctoral student, exploring some of the pains and pleasures, and does not focus extensively on practical matters such as examinations. It is premised on the notion of the PhD as a joint exploration by the student and supervisor rather than the PhD as just another qualification.

Index